journey to
.rt is

LARA
the Runaway Cat

DION LEONARD
with SOPHIE PEMBROKE

LARA
the Runaway Cat

One cat's journey to discover
home is where the heart is

HARPER
element

HarperElement
An imprint of HarperCollins*Publishers*
1 London Bridge Street
London SE1 9GF

www.harpercollins.co.uk

First published by HarperElement 2019
This edition 2019

3 5 7 9 10 8 6 4

A catalogue record of this book is
available from the British Library

ISBN 978-0-00-831627-3

Printed and bound in Great Britain by
CPI Group (UK) Ltd, Croydon, CR0 4YY

*This book is dedicated to cats and
their human slaves all around the world.*

Chapter
One

Humans are fickle. And easily led. At least, that's my experience.

Picture, if you will, a perfect specimen of cat-kind. A beautiful Ragdoll cat, with dark face and paws and fluffy white fur all over. An intelligent, stylish cat who looks after your house, keeps your knees warm at night, has refined tastes, hardly ever wanders or gets lost, and generally adds a sense of elegance to your life.

That's me: Lara.

Now, picture a stray dog, picked up in the Chinese desert, with ears that point almost directly *outwards* for goodness' sake, who scampers along with you, wins her way into your heart then manages to get completely lost, resulting in you having to go back to China to search for her. *Then* imagine that you want to bring the dog home to Britain with you, but that means you have to live in another country away from your perfect cat – and your wife, actually – for months on end because of some rules about animal travel. Basically, imagine a scruffy dog that causes all sorts of trouble by having *adventures*.

That's Gobi. My new sister pet, ever since Dad arrived home with her, 18 months ago.

I mean, really! Which would you prefer? It's an easy choice, right?

Apparently not so easy as you'd think.

Ever since Dad brought Gobi into our lives it has been constant chaos.

I don't like chaos, I like prawns for supper and quiet, predictable days.

Before Gobi came, all of my days were quiet and predictable. Ever since Mum and Dad brought me home as a kitten, from where I was born in Lancashire, more than 10 years ago now, my days have followed a pattern. Breakfast, cuddles, watching the world go by through the window, lunch, nap, play, more world-watching at my window, dinner, helping Dad watch TV by offering a constant commentary, supper, then sleep. And maybe middle-of-the-night snuggles if I felt them necessary (whatever Mum and Dad's feelings on the subject).

There was the odd bit of variety, I suppose, but all of it familiar. Comfortable.

For instance, sometimes, if I was feeling energetic, for a while I might chase a ball or my catnip toy – elegantly, of course – or a moth. And if I felt the need for an adventure, it was easy to follow Mum and Dad into the garden to smell the flowers and chew the grass.

In fact, the biggest adventure I ever had was the time I hid under the house (because squeezing into small places is fun, right?). *I* thought it was a game, but apparently it took Mum and Dad a while to catch on. Even then, it turns out they're rubbish at hide and seek because they could not find me. I could hear them calling, but they never even got anywhere close.

(Then I discovered – too late – that I was a bit stuck, and I had to meow *really* loudly to call them to me. It was dark and cold and I was hungry and lonely. I do not recommend it as a fun game for all the family.)

The point is, I never even dreamed about going any further than under the house. Why would I need to, when everything I wanted was right here at home?

But that was before Gobi.

The thing about Gobi is, everyone thinks she's fantastic. Special. A miracle of dog-kind.

(I think it's because of the book all about her. People think if you've had a book written about you, you're important. But of course, *Dad* wrote that book, not Gobi. If Gobi had actually written the book, maybe I'd have been more impressed.)

I'm not denying that Gobi has led a more varied life – more adventures, more trouble, more chaos.

I mean, yes, she ran through the Gobi Desert with Dad when he was doing his ultramarathon there, a few years ago. I *suppose* that takes some sort of talent. Dad's always talking about the training it takes, the physical and mental strength, that sort of thing. And I'm pretty sure I wouldn't want to do it. So, okay, we can give Gobi some sort of credit for running long distances.

And yes, okay, she also survived getting lost in China, after the race was done, before Dad could bring her home. Mum and Dad were so, so worried about her. Nobody knew where she was or what had happened to her. Of course, at that point, Mum and I hadn't met her, we'd only seen photos, but somehow it already felt like we knew her. Some people say she ran away, but I know the truth, even if Gobi doesn't like to talk about it. Somehow she kept herself alive until Dad could find her again.

That's how Gobi got famous – when Mum and Dad started a campaign on the Internet to find her and bring her home. It worked, sort of, even if she couldn't come home immediately because of some stupid rule about where and when pets can travel. Still, I suppose Dad wouldn't have spent all those months in China with her if she wasn't a *bit* important. Or been so excited when they were finally allowed to come home and we were suddenly a family of four, instead of three.

Lots of other people were excited too, it seems, as many of them wrote to tell us how happy they were for us.

Really? Fan mail? For a *dog*? She can't even read!

(Neither can I, yet, but I imagine it's only a matter of time before that skill comes to me. Most things do – I'm a very accomplished cat.)

The worst part about having Gobi in our lives isn't the fans, though. The worst part is Mum and Dad: they *adore* Gobi.

Before Gobi came, they talked to me, or about me. I was the centre of their world, and I liked being there. I knew exactly how important I was.

Until Dad met Gobi.

Now, they're always talking about how special *Gobi* is, how strong and brave, how well behaved. And they keep taking her on new adventures – without me.

In fact, *Gobi* goes on adventures with them every single day. A walk along the street or into the countryside with Mum and Dad, leaving me to watch them disappear from the window. Or sometimes, they go even further. I hear them talking about planes and ferries and distant lands and cities I've only seen if Dad's watching TV when I'm trying to talk to him.

Sometimes, Gobi even appears *on* the TV. That's the worst! Mum comes and grabs me to make me watch, like I want to see my sister doing all these things I could never get to do. The furthest I've got to an adventure is being allowed out along the side of the road on my harness on a long car trip to somewhere else. I'll sit behind a window and watch other people adventuring.

My whole life, I've watched the world through windows. That's what I do, you see. I'm a Ragdoll cat, and Ragdolls are indoor cats, so mostly I stay indoors. (Sometimes I venture as far as the garden, or in the car on a harness if Mum and Dad have to drive a long way away.) I watch the outside world go by, but I'm not supposed to want to be out there too. Not supposed to imagine what might be beyond the window frame. And until Gobi arrived, that was fine by me.

But now … now, sometimes I can't help but wonder what else might be out there. What draws Dad and Mum and Gobi out on their adventures? After all, what's the point of all the adventuring that other animals and humans do? I mean, they wouldn't do it if it wasn't important, or fun, right? So, I wonder. And I imagine.

What would my life be like if I was an *outdoor* cat, instead of an indoor one? If I went further than the garden wall one day? If, instead of hiding under the house, I went out beyond it?

Especially on the nights when Gobi steals my prawns, or gets excited and knocks me over, or even starts nibbling my tail. The nights when I remember what it was like when there were only three members of our family, and I was the most important one. I wonder what would happen if *I* decided to have an adventure.

But Ragdoll cats aren't made for the outside.

Or so I always thought.

The trees outside my window were blooming with spring blossoms the day I first got the idea for my own adventure. I remember, because I liked chasing the blossoms in the garden when they fell. They were light and fun and they floated along on the breeze, filling me with excitement.

Normally, anyway.

This year, I just watched them blow over the garden wall into the great outdoors beyond, and felt depressed that I couldn't follow them. So, I stayed inside instead, turning my back on the window and ignoring them.

Mum and Dad were talking about Gobi, *again*, and I was sort of half listening, half playing with a ball of fluffy hair (my own, of course) that had formed under the kitchen table.

'Well, if they want to interview you with Gobi, why don't we all go?' Mum said, sounding totally reasonable. 'Make a holiday of it. It would be nice to go back to China with you both.'

I glanced up at them. They were *all* going away this time? Last time Dad was in China, he was gone for months.

Already, I didn't like this plan.

Dad had his long legs stretched out under the table, but his expression wasn't nearly as relaxed as his position. 'I don't know. Is it wrong that just taking Gobi to China again makes me feel nervous?'

Of course it did – look at all the trouble she'd got into the last time she was there. Maybe they should stop letting Gobi out on adventures altogether, I thought. That might solve the problem.

And I wouldn't feel so left behind.

'She's not going to get lost again this time, Dion,' Mum said, soothingly. 'Besides, if we're all there together, we can look after each other.'

'I suppose.' Dad still didn't look convinced. I brushed up against his legs to remind him of my existence. It worked. 'What about Lara?' he asked, sitting up straight so I could jump up into his lap. 'We'd have to be away for weeks, to do the whole tour. I don't feel comfortable with the idea of leaving her for so long.'

Good. Neither did I.

'Then we'll take her with us!' Mum sounded strangely excited at the idea. Maybe she thought she'd been missing out on some adventures, too.

Personally, I was considerably wary of the whole idea. I mean, I'd never been *anywhere* before, and now they wanted to start off with *China*? I might not have travelled, but Dad had a map on the wall with pins showing all the places he and Mum and Gobi had travelled to. He'd pointed China out to me one day.

It was a *long* way across the map from my house.

'For the whole tour? Three weeks travelling around China, doing interviews, appearing at bookshops and so on …' Dad shook his head. 'I'm not sure how she'd cope with all that travel and fuss. She's more of a homebody, our Lara.'

'Hmm, I suppose she hasn't really been *anywhere* before, has she?' Mum agreed.

Even though I'd just had the exact same thought, my ears flattened to hear Mum say it, and my tail started to wave warningly from side to side. I would cope *magnificently*, of course, with whatever it was they were talking about doing. Really, Dad should know better than to suggest I couldn't do something! Just because I never had didn't mean I couldn't. It only meant that it had been below my notice before now.

Before Gobi, at least. Because things were very different, now.

Suddenly, all the things I'd been before Gobi – an indoor cat, a pampered princess, a fluffy homebody – they didn't sound like good things any more.

'She's just not an *adventurous* sort of pet,' Dad said, pressing the point home. 'Not like Gobi.'

It was those last three words that made my mind up. If Gobi could do it, so could I. And I'd do it better and cleverer, and with more panache too.

I'd be the most adventurous pet anyone had ever had, if that's what Mum and Dad wanted me to be.

I focussed in on their conversation. It always takes more effort to understand humans talking than other animals. But sometimes you have to put the work in to stay on top of what's going on.

Dad was talking about a tour – like the ones he and Gobi had been on before, around Britain, and overseas too. Gobi had travelled almost *everywhere* with Dad, while I'd stayed home in Edinburgh. I'd stared out of my window and waited for them to come back, when Dad would stick another pin in their map. Somewhere else they had been and I hadn't.

But this time, I had the chance to go, too. To find out what an adventure was really like.

I wasn't going to pass that up.

Dad petted my head, and noticed my flattened ears. 'I'm not sure Lara likes the idea, anyway.'

Honestly, humans! Do they understand nothing?

I meowed loudly and jumped up onto the table. Maybe Mum would understand more.

'I don't know,' she said, stroking my fluffy fur. 'She's always the first one into the suitcases whenever we go anywhere. Maybe she's been longing to take a trip with us all this time.'

I purred in agreement. Okay, my desire for travel was only a few minutes old, and I only usually climbed in the suitcases because they were filled with warm and soft things for snuggling on, but still … It was closer than Dad's interpretation, anyway.

'Okay, say we do this, how would it work?' Dad stood up, crossing to the kettle to make himself a drink. I followed, just in case he opened the fridge and there was anything interesting in there for me.

'Well, we could all take the ferry to France together, so Lara and Gobi don't have to travel in the hold of the plane leaving the UK,' said Mum, obviously thinking things through as she made up her plan on the spot. 'The overnight one, maybe, for a change? To break up the journey a bit. Then we can fly from France to China with the animals with us. We'd need to book pet-friendly accommodation everywhere anyway, for Gobi, so adding Lara into the mix won't make much difference for the hotels. And we can all explore the country together. It'll be fun!'

It did sound *sort of* fun, I supposed. Apart from the 'with Gobi' bit. I'd seen pictures of planes, and I knew they had windows. And Dad and Gobi sometimes videocalled from hotels when they were travelling, and they didn't look all that much different from the bedrooms at home.

But most of all, it *was* an adventure. Maybe I'd finally find out what all the fuss was about, and why people wanted to have them in the first place.

'What about when Gobi and I are doing interviews, or book signings and events and stuff?' Dad asked. Because of course, it was still all about Gobi. *Everything* was.

'Lara and I will come, too! Come on, Dion! You and Gobi have been *everywhere* together – the States, Canada …'

'Holland, Italy, France and Switzerland,' he added, in case we'd forgotten quite how many places they'd been together. Like we didn't have the map to remind us.

'Exactly. Maybe it's Lara's turn for an adventure.' Mum didn't say 'and mine too', but I got the feeling she was thinking it. 'Besides, it would be so nice to spend the summer all together as a family.'

That was true. Even if I wasn't completely thrilled that our family was made up of four of us now instead of three, I *really* didn't like the idea of the other three going off and having fun together and leaving me behind all summer.

'It *would* be nice,' Dad admitted. Reaching down, he picked me up and held me against his shoulder. 'What do you think, Lara? Would you like to come on an adventure with us?'

Most importantly, if I could show Mum and Dad that I was just as good at adventures as Gobi was – better even – maybe they'd remember that I was their favourite pet and quite clearly the superior animal in our household.

Even if I wasn't entirely sure what having an adventure entailed, yet. If Gobi could do it, how hard could it really be, anyway?

So, I meowed my agreement. Loudly. It was *my* turn to travel with Dad for a change.

Mum laughed, looking pleased, and Dad smiled too. For one precious moment, it was just the three of us again – and it was perfect.

Of course, Gobi picked that moment to wander into the kitchen, looking sleepy. She'd obviously just woken up from her afternoon nap, and arrived just in time to butt in on *my* important moment with Mum and Dad. As usual.

Dad put me down and went to make a fuss of Gobi instead. I slunk back to my ball of fluff again.

'Guess what, girl?' Dad said, sounding excited for the first time in the conversation. 'We're all going on an adventure. Together!'

Gobi barked her approval of the plan. I just hoped that they had prawns in China. And that I didn't have to share them with *Gobi*.

Chapter
Two

The planning for our trip took a lot more work than I'd expected. Before, I hadn't really paid much attention to what went into getting Gobi and Dad ready to go away. This time, though, I watched every detail, usually from inside a suitcase, where I couldn't possibly get forgotten. After a lifetime of happily staying inside, I was suddenly terrified of being left behind and missing out on the adventure.

With every day that passed, the excitement and anticipation grew in my belly – closely matched by the worry and the fear. Dad was wrong, obviously, about me not being able to cope with adventure. But that didn't change the fact that I'd never actually had one before, only heard about theirs.

In my experience, new things could be either very good (like the new, bigger prawns Mum had found for me) or very bad (like Gobi's dog biscuits, which *tasted* good, but always ended up with me being sick, every single time. I kept trying though, just in case).

I really hoped that adventures were more like prawns. But that didn't stop the nervousness from growing, especially as I learned more about the tour, where we were going, and what would be happening while we were away.

'I've got the itinerary through from the publishers,' Dad said one day, waving a few sheets of paper stapled together at us.

'Let's hear it then,' said Mum, as she put my prawns in my bowl.

I was torn: prawns or listening to the details of our adventure? In the end, I tried to do both. The prawns were delicious, as always; the itinerary less lovely.

In summary, the plan for our three weeks in China seemed to be: take Gobi to lots of lovely places, where there would be lots of people wanting to see her and make a fuss of her, wherever we went. And nobody to pay any attention at all to me, or *my* big adventure.

And that was the big problem: this was supposed to be my chance to show Mum and Dad that I was more than just an indoor cat, that I could be adventurous, too. But it still seemed very much like *Gobi's* adventure, even though I was along for the ride. How was I going to prove that I was the superior pet if everything was still about Gobi?

I sat at my window and ignored the world outside for once, thinking hard instead. There had to be a way to have my *own* adventure, surely? One that was all about me.

I just didn't know enough about adventures yet to figure out how.

By the time the day finally came to leave Edinburgh for Portsmouth and the ferry (via London, for some important, last-minute publisher meeting for Dad and Gobi), I'd started to go off the whole idea, really. I sulked in my carrier in the car, dozing off as we drove.

And when I saw the ferry, lit up brightly against the darkening night sky, I was *certain* this was a very bad idea indeed.

'It's huge!' I stared at the giant ship up ahead of us. It was bigger than our house, by far. I'd never even *seen* anything so big. Travelling by car was one thing – I quite enjoyed a car trip – I wasn't convinced I was going to enjoy *this* journey.

Gobi barked her agreement. 'Isn't it brilliant?'

'Brilliant' wasn't *quite* the word I'd been looking for.

'How long are we going to be on it?' I asked, still eyeing the ferry suspiciously.

'All night!' Gobi said it like that was a good thing.

Was the ferry the adventure? Because really, if we had that whole giant ship to explore, what more adventure could we possibly need? Maybe we should just turn around and go home – after all, Ragdoll cats were *indoor* cats. Not ferry cats or aeroplane cats or even China cats. I missed my window. And my prawns.

But just then, Dad put me in my carrier to take me aboard, and going home was no longer an option.

Adventures also seemed to involve a lot of people frowning at paperwork. Before we were even allowed on the ferry, a man had to glare at some paper, then run the same magic device thing over me that they sometimes used at the vet's.

'That's to make sure we're who we say we are,' Gobi told me, from where she was being checked at the next table.

I hunkered down back inside my carrier and glowered. I wasn't enjoying being in Gobi's world. At home, I knew everything and she didn't. Where the warmest spots to curl up were. Where Mum hid the dog treats. The best blankets for snuggling on. The ideal time to interrupt Dad's programmes when he was watching TV. How *not* to get trapped underneath the house playing hide and seek.

When Gobi had arrived home with Dad, I'd had to teach her *everything* about our home, our lives, our family. Here, things seemed to be the other way around.

It wasn't natural.

Once we were on the ferry itself, I started to feel more at home. Mum and Dad had booked us something called a 'pet-friendly cabin'. (I didn't want to know what made the other cabins unfriendly towards pets.) It had two narrow beds, a window, and a door that opened onto a small bathroom. As soon as Dad let me out of my carrier, I hopped up onto the little table under the window to look out.

I'd hoped it would feel familiar, like all the other windows I'd stared out of over the years. Instead, I looked out over an expanse of endless water, and shuddered.

It looked hundreds of times worse than bathtime.

Behind me, Mum laughed. 'Don't worry, Lara. You're safe in here, the water can't reach you.'

But I wasn't about to take her word for it, so I jumped back down onto the bed and made myself at home.

Dad was standing in the open doorway, moving a bag from the hall into our cabin, when another lady appeared outside, with another pet carrier. She smiled at Dad as she passed, then she stopped, stared inside our cabin, and her grin grew even larger.

'Look, Cleo! Another Ragdoll, just like you! And staying right next door to us. How lovely to meet fellow discerning pet lovers! It can be so lonely travelling alone.' She lifted her carrier so her cat – Cleo, I presumed – could see me. We surveyed each other with steady gazes. I couldn't get a really good look at her, behind the bars of her carrier door, but if she was a Ragdoll like me, I was sure she must be gorgeous.

When I tuned back into the human conversation again, Mum was saying, 'Would you like a drink? Dion was just going to pop to the cafe for a hot chocolate for me,' to Cleo's human and, before I knew it, Cleo was out of her carrier and onto the bed with me.

'Ooh, that sounds be lovely! I'm Jennifer, by the way.' Cleo's human bustled into the already cramped cabin, and took a seat on the end of my bed.

I meowed a welcome to Cleo. 'I'm Lara. And the dog is Gobi,' I added, jerking my head towards my sister pet.

'Cleo,' the other Ragdoll said, not even acknowledging Gobi. I liked her already.

'I'll just go find the cafe then,' Dad said, looking bemused. It was just as well he left – he's a tall guy, and the cabin really wasn't all that big for all six of us.

'So, are you off to France on holiday?' Mum asked, settling onto the other bed. Gobi was already asleep beside her. It was very late, I supposed, but I'd slept so much in the car down, I wasn't tired at all. (I don't know what it is about car journeys, but they always send me to sleep. I was hoping the ferry might do the same, but already there were so many strange noises and smells, I wasn't sure I'd be able to settle.)

'No, just passing through,' Jennifer said. 'We're flying out of Paris tomorrow.'

'Us too!' said Mum. 'We wanted to have the animals with us on the plane.' And we wanted to be there with them. I still remembered Gobi's tales of travelling in the hold of a plane in China. I shuddered just thinking about them.

Jennifer nodded. 'Exactly! I really don't like to fly without Cleo. And until Britain lets animals travel with passengers instead of in the hold, I will *only* fly out of Paris.'

At the other end of the bed, Cleo rolled her eyes, and settled her head down on her paws. I padded closer – other cats were usually far more interesting to talk to than humans.

'You don't look very excited to be going on this trip.' I took a spot close enough to Cleo to talk, but not so close as to crowd her, and began nonchalantly licking my leg.

'You wouldn't be either, if you were travelling with her.' Cleo jerked her head in the direction of Jennifer, sitting behind her.

'Oh, look!' Jennifer clapped her hands together and beamed. 'They're talking to each other!'

Mum smiled, too. 'Oh, Lara's quite the chatterbox. Especially when Dion is trying to watch the sports. He says she always seems to know exactly when something important is about to happen, and then she interrupts.'

Cleo ignored them, so I did too.

'She seems … enthusiastic,' I said, eyeing Jennifer carefully.

'That's one word for it.' With a sigh, Cleo heaved herself closer, as if she needed to whisper so Jennifer wouldn't hear what she was saying. Like humans would ever concentrate long enough to understand *us* the way we understand them. 'She gets so excited about things, she forgets what *really* matters: me.'

'I know how that feels.' I glanced across at Gobi on the other bed. She was Mum and Dad's latest excitement. And maybe they hadn't forgotten about me completely, but they'd definitely stopped remembering that *I* was the most important animal in their lives.

'She always has to be doing something too,' Cleo went on, obviously pleased to have someone to moan to about her human. 'She got really into crystals last year. Kept trying to use these pieces of rock to cure me.'

'What was wrong with you?'

'Nothing,' Cleo said, mournfully. 'Well, except for when she dropped a huge piece of quartz on my tail.'

I winced, and put a paw over my face – that *did* sound painful.

'The worst part,' Cleo went on, 'is the adventures.'

'Adventures?' My ears pricked up at that – even if Cleo did say it like it was one of those words Mum scolded Dad for using sometimes.

'Yeah. Ever since her husband, Jeremy, died, she's been running around all over the world.'

'Why?' That was the part I still didn't fully understand about adventures – why people wanted to have them. I mean, I knew why *I* needed to have one, but presumably everyone else wasn't also having them to prove superiority over a dog. So, what was so special about them? So far, it just seemed like I was looking out of a different window from normal. Nothing much else had changed, except that I had to eat one of those horrible pouches of food for my dinner instead of my usual fresh prawns.

I was certain I was missing something about adventures. If this was all there was, I really couldn't understand why people wanted to have them at all.

'Something about finding the perfect place to scatter his ashes.'

'Ashes?'

'That's what was left of Jeremy, after he died,' Cleo explained.

'And now she needs to put them somewhere else? Why?'

'I have no idea. But I heard them talking before he went into hospital the last time. She said she'd find him his ideal place to spend eternity.' Cleo shrugged her shoulders, then stretched out her paws in front of her. 'All I know is that she's dragging me all over the world, and she's a *terrible* flyer. That's why she needs to take me with her. Apparently, I'm her ESA.'

'What's an ESA?' Could I be one? Well, if it turned out to be a good thing, anyway.

'Emotional Support Animal,' Cleo explained. 'Means she grips tight hold of me whenever a plane is taking off or landing, and talks to me constantly in between when I'm trying to nap.'

I'd never been on a plane, or any further away from home than I was right now. But I would tomorrow. I'd be flying high in the sky over to China, according to Mum. I wondered if they'd hold tight to me.

I looked over at Gobi again. Mum had one hand resting on her fur as she talked to Jennifer. And I knew, right then, that I wasn't anyone's ESA: *Gobi* was. She was the pet who had changed everything. The one who got to go on all the big adventures, because people wanted to see her wherever she went. I was just tagging along. This wasn't my big trip at all, it was all Gobi's.

'And this is going to be her longest journey yet.' Cleo was still talking, oblivious to my realization of my unimportance. 'She's going all the way to Australia. That's practically a whole day on a plane, she says. And …' Cleo's voice dropped, lower and smaller, like she was ashamed of what she was going to say next. '… I'm terrified of flying. It was bad enough just jetting around Europe but a whole day on a plane? I can't take it. All I want is to go back home, with the automatic kitty feeder they used to use when they went away for a weekend. Is that so much to ask?'

I made a vague sympathetic noise, but my brain was stuck on one word.

Australia.

I knew about Australia. Not much, but enough.

You see, that was where Dad was from, before he met Mum and me. He grew up there. He showed me on the map – and it was further away than China, even.

Dad talked about Australia sometimes. Not often, but every now and again. Because he'd not been back there in years – since long before he found Gobi in the desert.

Which meant that *Gobi* had never been to Australia.

That was an adventure that was too much even for Gobi.

But I was sure I could do it.

I studied Cleo carefully. Same fluffy white and dark brown fur. Same blue eyes. Same fluffy tail. We really did look very alike …

Suddenly, an idea floated into my mind. An adventurous, crazy idea. One that was more extreme than a ferry ride, or a book tour. It might even be more exciting than being lost in China, or running an ultramarathon.

The sort of idea that, if it worked, would mean that *no one* would be able to say that I was just an indoor, homebody cat ever again.

I'd be Lara, cat adventurer. *I'd* be the pet everyone wanted to talk about. Maybe they'd even write a book about me, too.

'We should swap places,' I said, without thinking it through any further. 'I'll go to Australia with Jennifer, and you can …' Ah … For a cat who hated flying, I was pretty sure the flight to China wouldn't be a lot of fun, either.

'Hide out in the airport until Jennifer gives up and comes home again?' Cleo finished for me. She sat up straighter, looking imperious and calculating. Somehow, I got the feeling that my adventure had just slipped from my paws into hers. 'That could work.'

'It *could*?' I'll be honest, I hadn't thought through the specifics, I'd just acted on impulse. Like Gobi did.

To my surprise, it felt kind of good.

'We'd need to be cunning about it.' Cleo was watching Jennifer again, sounding thoughtful. 'But yes, I think it could work.'

'Great,' I said. But inside I was wondering what on earth I'd got myself into now. It had sounded exciting in my head, but now the words were out in the world, it was sort of, kind of, terrifying.

Well, I'd wanted my own adventure. One that wasn't about Gobi at all.

It looked like I'd got one.

Chapter
Three

J ust as Dad returned to the cabin with hot chocolates, I asked
Cleo, 'Okay, so how would this work?'

We both stopped chatting to pay attention to our humans
again for a moment.

'Oh, Dion, Jennifer and Cleo are headed to the airport same
as us tomorrow morning. We've got space to give them a lift,
right?' Mum said, taking her paper cup.

Dad shrugged. 'Sure, happy to help.'

My dad is too nice sometimes – I reckon that's how we
ended up with Gobi. But on this occasion, it suited my plans
perfectly.

'That makes things a lot easier.' Cleo stretched out her paws
in front of her, arching her back as she thought. I could
almost see the plan forming behind her calculating blue eyes.
Finally, she settled back down again and said, 'Here's what we'll
do.'

I shuffled up closer to listen. I'd had the grand idea, but was
definitely going to need help with the details.

'The key is all in the timing,' Cleo said. I got the feeling that
she liked to pontificate – something Dad said I always did when
he was watching the sport. Still, under the circumstances, I was
willing to put up with a bit of fellow cat know-it-all-ness. 'We
can't make the swap until after they check our pet passports and
microchips.'

'Of course,' I murmured, even though I was actually thinking,
I have a passport? I mean, I knew about the microchip thingy,
buried under my fur, but I'd never needed a passport before. (I'd

seen Dad's, though. He looked *hilarious* in the photo, and Mum liked to show it around any friends who stopped by, whenever he was preparing for another trip.)

'Once we've been checked, but *before* we go our separate ways, we need to switch places, without anyone noticing.'

'Easy,' I said, although actually, it sounded anything but. I tried to picture how it would work, but without ever having been to an airport before, or gone through the security things Gobi had talked about, I couldn't imagine it. Would it be like getting on the ferry, with the man who scowled at paperwork? Or would it be totally different?

If our humans weren't looking too closely, they might not notice if we swapped places. I hoped …

'We'll see,' Cleo replied. I supposed she was right – I'd have to wait and see how it all worked.

But one thing I was certain of – it *would* work. It had to. This was my one chance to escape on a real adventure, not just tagging around after Gobi. I wasn't going to miss it.

I raised my head, stretching out my neck as I sat, imperious. 'It'll work like clockwork, just wait and see. We'll swap places, and I'll go adventuring to Australia with Jennifer, and you can …' The gap in my plan suddenly seemed obvious. 'Wait, what are you really going to do once we've swapped?' I didn't think she'd want to fly to China with Mum and Dad, but what other choice would she have?

But Cleo just shrugged. 'I'll hang out with your people long enough for you to make your getaway, then I'll lose them before we get on the plane.'

'Lose them? How? You'll be in my carrier.' And I had tried opening that door from the inside before, usually when they were using it to take me to the vet. It didn't work.

But Cleo looked unconcerned by the difficulties ahead. 'Yowl loud enough and someone will open the door eventually. Then I just need to slip past them and make a run for it.'

'What if you get caught? And, actually, what if you don't? What will you do?' It sounded to me like Cleo had her own adventure planned.

'If I can stay free, I'll just hide out around the airport as long as it's fun and entertaining. Then, when I'm ready for humans again, I'll let myself get caught by the airport staff. They'll just check my microchip, then put me up in some pet hotel or another until Jennifer gets back in the country. Hopefully, losing me will put her off flying for a while.'

For someone planning an audacious escape, Cleo seemed remarkably calm and unruffled. Were her nerves jangling like mine were, inside? If she hated flying as much as she said, she must be a bit nervous, right? I wished she'd show it – it would make me feel better.

And there was something else Cleo hadn't considered, either.

'Unless Jennifer decides she likes me better, and wants to keep me.' I was hoping to ruffle her, just a little bit. But Cleo just laughed, which was rather insulting.

I got the feeling that Cleo wasn't really that nice a cat. But she was helping me, so I'd need to put up with her, for now at least.

Later, once Jennifer had whisked Cleo back into her carrier to take her next door, and Mum and Dad were ready for bed, Gobi settled down next to me and asked, 'What were you and your lookalike whispering about earlier?'

I allowed myself a small, smug smile. 'You'll have to wait and see.'

'I didn't like her,' Gobi said. 'She seemed sly. Sneaky. Not like you.'

If only Gobi knew how sneaky I could be, when I needed to. But it was better that she didn't. Mum and Dad and Gobi were all so convinced that I was a boring, homebody cat, they'd never even dream I could plan an adventure like this, so they'd never see it coming. I'd be halfway to Australia before they even realized what had happened.

It was the perfect plan.

I smiled to myself, and curled up, my paws under my chin and my tail wrapped over Gobi's back to try to sleep. But without the distractions of Cleo and Jennifer, or making plans, I was very aware that I was on the giant ship in the middle of more water than I'd ever imagined could exist, even when Dad pointed out the oceans on his map.

Gobi was already snoring, so I hopped off the bed and over to the little table under the window, almost knocking over Mum's bottle of water. Pressing my paws against the window, I looked outside again.

The waves rose and fell around us, making even the huge ferry sway from side to side. The moon glowed in the sky, and again in the water. I knew from Dad's documentaries that it was the same moon that looked down on our house in Edinburgh, the same moon my family would see in China, and the same moon I'd be looking at in Australia.

The whole wide world to explore, but only one moon. That made me feel a little better about everything, somehow.

After a while, watching the waves started to make my stomach feel odd, so I settled down again next to Gobi, listening to her gentle snores, and Mum and Dad's breathing as they slept. This might be the last night I heard those sounds for a while, so

I drank them all in, storing the memory away for other nights, away from my family. After a while, they merged with the other sounds I could hear – creaks and clanks from the ferry, the voices of some of the other passengers passing our door, the waves outside lapping against the boat.

Eventually, I fell asleep to the sound of the waves rocking the boat, still picturing Gobi's face when she realized I was having a much bigger adventure than she ever could.

Airports turned out to be a lot bigger than I expected. And noisier.

There were so many people, everywhere, that I could see instantly how easy it would be for Cleo to lose herself among them, after I was gone. Once she'd escaped from the carrier, anyway.

So far, everything had gone perfectly to plan.

The ferry had docked early in the morning, and we'd all had breakfast together in our little cabin before we headed out to find our car again. Dad helped Jennifer with her cases too, taking her with us down to the car. We sat in the giant car park on the boat, and I peered out from my carrier through a sliver of window I could see, waiting to see the new country we'd arrived in – France.

Jennifer and Cleo travelled with us on the drive to the airport, Cleo in her carrier beside mine. We'd exchanged knowing looks, but hadn't risked discussing our plan with Gobi there to listen in. I wasn't sure how she'd stop us, but I was pretty sure she'd try, if she knew what we were planning. I reckoned Gobi liked being the only pet to have the big adventures.

My whole body buzzed with anticipation throughout the long drive to the airport – and for once, I didn't even fall asleep in the car! I was far too excited for that.

31

At the airport, Jennifer stuck with us, just as Cleo and I had hoped she would. I'd tried to imagine what we'd do if she decided to go her own way once we got there, but without being able to picture an airport, it was impossible.

Now I could see exactly what one looked like, it only seemed more so.

It helped that Cleo had talked me through what would happen – and that, actually, it wasn't very much different to the systems we'd been through at the ferry port the day before. Now, though, I realized that the papers Dad handed over to the man in the uniform were probably mine and Gobi's passports – for all they looked different to his and Mum's.

Nobody seemed all that interested in us, except to scan our microchips and glance at our papers. Except, of course, for the overly chatty security man, who recognized Gobi from the telly.

'I can't believe she really ran all that way through the desert with you!' he said, as he checked Gobi's passport. Gobi preened at the attention, as usual.

'She really did.' Dad ruffled Gobi's scruffy, sandy fur. As if mine wasn't a hundred times softer and fluffier and overall much, much nicer to ruffle. 'She's a born adventurer, this one!'

I hunkered down in my soft carrier, waiting for someone to remember that I was there, more determined than ever to show my humans that *I* could have an adventure even better than Gobi's. And I wouldn't feel the need to brag about it on TV all the time, either. Although, if my public came calling, of course I wouldn't want to disappoint them either. And a book deal would be nice …

Finally, we were through security, and Dad took Gobi out of her carrier and popped her lead on instead. Mum reached into the bag she had on her back and pulled out my harness – the one she uses when we go on long car journeys and I need to stretch my legs at the side of the road. My eyes widened with panic as I saw it in her hand.

We hadn't planned for harnesses.

Just behind us, Cleo and Jennifer were exiting security, too, and I tried to catch Cleo's eye through the door of her carrier. Once the harness was on, there was no way I could escape and still be mistaken for Cleo afterwards. My harness is, let's say, distinctive. (It's bright pink, with yellow and orange flowers on it. Dad chose it – for the record, he said it was a joke. Mum said it would definitely make it less likely that anyone would try to steal me, so she insists on using it every time we go anywhere in the car, now.)

Mum was still untangling the harness lead as Jennifer put Cleo's carrier on the floor, just across from mine. Perfect! Catching her eye, I meowed my concerns across to her, but Cleo merely smiled.

'Just wait for my signal,' she said.

Her signal? How would I know what her signal was? We definitely hadn't discussed signals when we were planning the night before. What if I screwed up my one chance at an adventure because I didn't recognize the signal? Didn't Cleo know I was new to all this?

But then, as I was quietly fretting, Mum knelt down to open my carrier. The moment the door clicked open, Cleo started making the most almighty racket, yowling and clawing at the material of her carrier.

Oh. That was probably the signal. It was kind of hard to miss.

I pushed my paw against the door to my carrier: Mum had left it open! And she was distracted – as was everyone in the immediate area – by Cleo's crying and fussing. There was no one to spot what *I* was doing. I slipped out of the carrier easily, and crossed to where Jennifer was opening Cleo's carrier to find out what the problem was. Nobody noticed me – as usual.

Cleo shot out the moment the door was opened, and raced across to me, blending our fur together as we wound around each other. From outside our cat spiral, it must have been nearly impossible to tell which fur belonged to which cat – we really were a perfect match. It made me think this whole adventure was meant to be.

'Lara!' Mum admonished, as she reached down to grab me. 'You know better than to run away.'

Did I? I'd never even *thought* about running before this trip. But now adventure was calling. This was my last chance to change my mind. My heart pounding, I thought about not running – about staying, and being second-place pet to Gobi the adventurer for the rest of my life – and made my decision easily.

I threw myself out of the way at the last minute as Mum's hands came down, and Cleo happily swung into my place. Mum wasn't even really looking – she was listening to Jennifer, who was saying, 'I'm so sorry! It's all Cleo's fault for upsetting her. I don't know *what* she's making such a fuss about!'

'I don't think we'll risk Lara out of the carrier for now anyway,' said Mum, holding Cleo tightly in both hands as she passed her to Dad. Then Mum tucked the harness away again in her bag, as Dad fastened the door on my carrier firmly – with Cleo inside.

I was right: I was so unimportant, they hadn't even noticed they had the wrong cat.

Part of me, I realized suddenly, had been hoping this wouldn't work. That Mum and Dad could *never* mistake another cat for their beloved Lara, however similar we looked.

But they had. And that made my adventure more important than ever.

'Come on!' I realized suddenly that Jennifer was trying to shoo me inside Cleo's carrier, her hands pressing against the fur on my rump. With one last look at my family, I went docilely, and hoped my agreeable nature didn't give me away too soon.

My little heart beat double time as the door closed. It was really happening, my adventure was here at last!

Outside, I could hear Gobi barking furiously. She was trying to warn them about the mistake they were making, I realized. Dad tried to calm her down, but nothing was working. She'd noticed our swap, even if none of the humans had. Our switch had gone flawlessly. And Gobi was probably just jealous that I was going on a bigger adventure than her.

Luckily, Gobi had never learned to communicate with humans properly either. They'd never figure out what she was saying in time to stop us.

And Gobi would get over it. She'd probably never even miss me when I was gone.

'Well, thank you so much for the lift to the airport,' Jennifer said, as she lifted me up. 'I'm sorry for this little ruckus! I'd better get Cleo safely to our gate before she causes any more trouble. Have a lovely time in China.'

'And enjoy Australia with your daughter,' said Mum. Through the carrier door, I could see her leaning in to hug Jennifer. And then we were moving away, away from my family, and everything I'd ever known before.

I craned my neck back to watch them as best I could through the slits in the carrier, drinking in my last sight of Mum, Dad and Gobi.

Then I turned around to face my future.

The adventure was on!

 # Gobi

My sister Lara is the best sister anyone could want. She lets me cuddle up to her at night if it's cold, or I'm lonely. She even wraps her tail over me to keep me warm. She shares her prawns with me, every single day. (I let her have some of my biscuits in return, but they always make her sick.) Lara is lovely to nibble on, with all that fluffy fur, and I miss her when I go away. She's always there waiting for me at the window when I get home again, though.

I never had anybody before I met Dion. He brought me home to meet Lucja and Lara and now I have more than three people.

I have a family. And that makes me the luckiest dog in the world.

Or it did.

I knew there was something wrong with Lara, something bothering her maybe, but I couldn't understand what it could be. She seemed restless, unhappy even. But how could any animal be unhappy with a family as great as ours?

I was apprehensive when Dion said we were going back to China. Usually, I like going on book tours with him. I like the interviews and the meeting people and the seeing new places. But China wasn't new, and the memories I had from my birthplace weren't nice.

Apart from meeting Dion. That was one of the best memories I had.

But the others ... My life in China hadn't been kind. Even running the marathon with Dion, while I'd loved the company and the excitement, had been hard. And everything that came after ... I tried very hard not to think about the time when Dion and I were separated, but sometimes I still got nightmares.

So, no. China would not have been my choice for our next adventure together.

But when I realized that Lucja and Lara would be coming along, too, that made things different. Going to China with my whole family, that was something else entirely.

A chance to let go of the past, perhaps. To chase away those nightmares and replace them with new dreams. Happier ones.

Besides, as long as we were all together, I knew nothing bad could happen to me.

Not this time. Not with my sister there to protect me.

Except now I was very afraid she wouldn't be.

It was all the fault of that other cat, I knew it. Cleo, that was her name. She'd been whispering things in Lara's ear all the previous evening, and while I didn't know what they were talking about, I knew I didn't like it. It had made Lara all secretive and aloof, the way she got sometimes when she was cross with me for something.

It made her act not like my sister.

Still, I didn't understand how dangerous Cleo was until we were at the airport, and the two of them made such a scene, winding around each other until ...

No. Oh no!

That was when I realized.

When Lucja picked up Cleo instead of my Lara and put her in the carrier.

Why couldn't they see what was happening? That awful cat had stolen Lara's place!

I didn't want another cat, I wanted Lara. And I knew Dion and Lucja would too, when they realized what had happened.

If only they'd listen to me …

I watched Cleo carefully through the bars of Lara's carrier. She looked very pleased with herself; she knew exactly what she'd done. Poor Lara, tricked by a fellow feline!

I kept trying to tell Dion what was going on, all the way to the gate. I've been through a lot of airports over the last year or two, and I know the drill. Normally, I sit quietly beside Dion, unless someone wants to make a fuss of me, when I stand up and let them pet me for a while.

Not today.

Today, I barked at Cleo, I ran circles around Dion's legs, trying to get his attention by tangling him up in my lead. I even jumped up onto Lucja's lap to try and get her to just look at the cat in the carrier, but she just thought I was after the snack she was eating, and ordered me back down.

Skulking around the carrier, I tried to figure out my next move.

'I don't know what's the matter with her today!' Dion said, reaching down to pat my head as I quivered with anger and fear at his feet.

Where was Lara? Would she ever come home again? What if she needed me?

'Maybe she just wants to be with Lara,' Lucja suggested, more spot on than she knew. 'Come on, we can probably let her out on the harness again now Cleo isn't here.'

She bent down and unfastened the door to Lara's carrier, the cat harness already in her hands. But before she had a chance to even slip it over the cat's head, Cleo shot past her, across the airport gate, weaving through the metal chair legs fixed to the ground.

I didn't think, I just chased.

If Lara was gone, I couldn't risk losing Cleo too. Not when she might be the only clue we had to help get Lara home, where she belonged.

I had to catch her.

I chased Cleo through the gate, back out into the main airport halls, weaving through people's legs and dodging suitcases as I went. As long as I kept her in my sight, I still had hope – hope that she would lead me back to the real Lara again.

I closed in on her as she approached a large group of travellers with huge suitcases on wheels. Finally, I thought I had her trapped. I added a last burst of extra speed to catch her – only for her to dodge away to the right at the last moment, leaving me barrelling into the middle of the suitcases, people cursing at me as I flailed, trying to find my paws.

The ground felt like it was moving beneath me – and it took me a moment to realize that it really was! Cleo had tricked me onto the travelator – the one Dion never let me walk on normally when we went through airports. Some of these things went on for miles, I remembered. I'd have lost that cat for sure by the time I got to the other end!

Determined, I fought my way out of the suitcases, and back towards the way I'd come from, racing against the moving floor with every step, and finally collapsing onto the smooth tiles at the far end.

'Did Gobi find her?' I heard Lucja's voice calling, and when I looked up, Dion was standing over me. At least they'd realized, then, what I was trying to do.

My heart sank as I realized the full implications of that.

They'd know that I'd failed.

That I had lost Lara. Even if it wasn't really her to begin with.

I rested my head on my paws and whined.

How could Dion and Lucja forgive me?

And how would we ever get Lara back now? Who would keep me safe in China, without my sister there to protect me?

39

Chapter
Four

Cleo hadn't been exaggerating when she said that Jennifer was a *terrible* flyer. No wonder she hadn't wanted to fly all the way to Australia with her.

Not having been on a plane before, I didn't have too many expectations of what flying would be like. And, to be honest, I'd been too busy focussing on how Cleo and I would effect our switch to concentrate on what would happen next. Even the flight to China with Mum and Dad and Gobi had been too far away to think about, when there were ferries and other adventures to experience first.

But now it was time to fly. And suddenly I realized that maybe I should have given a *little* more thought to this part of the plan earlier in the proceedings.

After sitting for ages in a row of chairs around many other rows of chairs somewhere that was called a 'gate' (but didn't have any metal doors, unlike the gate to our garden back home), there was some sort of tinny announcement that rang out around the area. I couldn't see who was talking, and it was hard to even make out the words that they were saying, but Jennifer leapt to her feet, the handle of my carrier in her hand. I lurched upwards too as she moved.

She joined a queue of other people, and I tried to look around me and take in my surroundings. There were plenty of windows here at the gate, too. Glass seemed to make up an entire wall of the building, at least on this level, and I could see out over a field of concrete – with large, white crafts with wings dotted around it.

Planes. Airplanes. That I'd be flying on. *Very* soon.

Birds flew, I knew that much. I'd seen them in the sky back home, and even chased one or two when I was exploring the garden – although I always had to give up when they escaped over the garden wall.

But now it was my turn. I wondered if there'd be any birds up there to catch …

Flying was an adventure, I was sure of that. But it was one Gobi had done lots of times before, so somehow it didn't really seem to count, yet. I kept remembering all the things she had told me about planes and flying, none of it particularly useful right now.

I couldn't wait to have an adventure Gobi had never experienced at all. To be the one who knew something about the wide world outside the window that Gobi didn't.

'Us next, Cleo.' Jennifer hoisted me up again, as the queue moved forwards. 'I hope Jeremy appreciates all I'm doing for him,' she muttered.

I wondered who Jeremy was, and why he wanted Jennifer to travel the world when she hated flying. Then I remembered what Cleo had said about Jennifer's dead husband, and finding a place for him to spend eternity. *His* name was Jeremy.

I hoped for Cleo's sake that Jennifer found the perfect place for his ashes on this trip. Otherwise Cleo would have more flights in her future, I was sure.

'Animals are required to remain in their carriers during the flight, Madam,' the flight attendant standing by the tall desk told us, as Jennifer showed her boarding card.

'Of course,' Jennifer replied, pleasantly. But the moment we were out of earshot she murmured, 'Don't listen to her, Cleo.

You'll be on my lap, like always. You know I can't fly without you! Goodness, I think my hands might be shaking already.'

There was no 'might' about it. My carrier was jiggling around like blossom blowing past our window in Edinburgh as we walked down a long corridor towards another door.

I almost didn't notice when we boarded the plane. It was just like going through another door – like the one between the hallway and the bedroom at home, even. Except suddenly the windows were much, much smaller, and the chairs were all fixed in place, in narrow rows. I wondered if I got my own seat – there wasn't going to be much room for me otherwise, in my carrier.

One thing I could tell for certain, as we made our way down the path in the middle of the plane, behind the seats – there were *plenty* of small places for a fluffy cat like me to hide, if I wanted to. I probably couldn't get *off* the plane once it was in the air, I supposed, but if Jennifer proved too annoyingly clingy, at least I could escape and hide somewhere else for a while, supposing she let me go long enough for me to run.

Our seat was almost halfway down the plane, next to a window. I liked that. I understood windows, and I liked to look out. Hopefully, once I was out of my carrier, like Jennifer had promised, I'd be able to take a good look around.

Really, it wasn't all that much different to home yet.

Jennifer settled into her seat comfortably, pulling out a magazine, a small pillow that tucked around her neck and a small bag of treats that I hoped were for me. Clearly, she knew just what a journey like this required – as Cleo had told me, she'd been doing this for a while.

I supposed Jennifer herself was another clue as to why people went on adventures. She was searching for something, the perfect place to scatter Jeremy's ashes. A bit like how Dad had adventured to China to find Gobi again, when she went missing.

I wondered what I was looking for, besides an actual adventure. Whatever it was, I hoped I would figure it out before I found it.

Another woman sat down beside Jennifer. A tall, thin woman with kind eyes, she smiled down at me, where I sat in my carrier, on the floor at Jennifer's feet.

Jennifer obviously noticed, because she said, 'Hello! This is Cleo, she's my Emotional Support Animal.'

I didn't correct her, obviously.

'She's beautiful,' the woman said, peering through the slits in my carrier. I preened, just a little bit. Ragdoll cats really *are* the most beautiful animals. 'Hello Cleo, I'm Caitlin.'

'And I'm Jennifer.' Jennifer leant in closer to Caitlin, and whispered, 'As soon as those stewardesses are sat down, I'll get her out to sit on my lap. Then you can get a proper look at her. She's a purebred Ragdoll, you know. A very special cat.'

'I'm sure she is.' The other woman didn't sound completely convinced that I was anything more special than a pretty cat, but then she hadn't met me properly yet. She'd understand in time.

Over the next few minutes, more and more people sat down in their seats, as the plane filled up. There were women and men in suits, with small, hard cases on wheels that they crammed into the boxes above the seats. There were families, with rucksacks and bags full of toys. There was at least one screaming baby that I hoped would go to sleep soon. And there were couples, holding hands and smiling as they found their seats.

And with every person who boarded the plane, Jennifer grew more and more agitated. I wasn't sure why, nothing had even happened yet. What was there to be afraid of?

Gobi had told me, before we left Edinburgh, that take-off and landing were the scariest parts of flying. But we hadn't taken off anywhere yet.

Jennifer was obviously panicking in anticipation, though. First, she pulled my carrier up fully onto her lap, instead of letting it sit at her feet. Then she started hugging it – her arms wrapped around and squashing the soft material. I could smell her sweat through her clothes.

Not a new favourite scent.

'Are you okay?' Caitlin asked, leaning forward with concern. 'Do you need me to call someone?'

'I'll be fine,' said Jennifer, unconvincingly. 'I've got Cleo, she makes it all bearable.'

'You don't like flying,' the woman realized. 'That's why you have your cat with you.'

'Of course! Why else?'

I caught a glimpse of the woman's face through the slits of my carrier. She looked vaguely uncomfortable, and I guessed she wasn't going to answer that question. I wondered what she'd assumed was wrong with Jennifer that she needed Cleo to go everywhere with her.

'Are you sure I can't get anything for you?' she persisted. 'Some water? A mint to suck on take-off?'

Clearly feeling guilty for whatever assumptions she'd jumped to.

'No, thank you,' Jennifer replied. 'I'll be fine once we get going. It's just this waiting, I do hate the waiting.'

But just then, the pilot's voice came over the intercom –

just like Gobi had told me it would, when she'd been lecturing me about everything that would happen on our trip, since she'd done it all before. She'd just been lording it over me, of course. Making it clear that anything I did, she'd already experienced.

But not this: this was *my* adventure with Jennifer.

'We are cleared for take-off,' the pilot said, and the plane started to move.

Jennifer gave a sharp squeak, like one of Gobi's toys when she's played with it too roughly, and before I knew what was happening, I was out of my carrier and wrapped up directly in Jennifer's arms. Just like the flight attendant had told her I shouldn't be.

Jennifer had a seat belt on. Outside of my carrier there was nothing at all to stop me hurtling through the plane on take-off. Well, nothing except Jennifer's very strong embrace.

Gobi hadn't mentioned Dad doing anything like this when *they* were flying.

Beside us, Caitlin made a soothing noise and patted Jennifer's arm. I don't know why she was bothering to try and soothe her when *I* was clearly the one in distress. *I* was the one with no security straps or cases, and who might actually be squeezed to death before we reached Australia anyway.

Jennifer started talking, murmuring nonsense in my ears, all about Jeremy and being without him and how he'd want her to go visit her daughter and stuff. I tuned her out – nothing to do with me, after all – and instead focussed on the view out of the window, as a distraction from the squeezing of my middle.

This window wasn't like any of the others I'd stared out of before. It was smaller, for a start, and rounded. But the newest part was the view.

As the plane tilted and rose, the ground sped away from us, the concrete river of the runway disappearing as we flew. Soon, I saw the green of trees and the roofs of houses below us, the blue of rushing water, and what I assumed had to be cars moving along roads – although they looked smaller than mice.

And then there was nothing but sky and clouds, for miles and miles.

Somehow, this wasn't as terrifying as the never-ending ocean we'd crossed on the ferry. This wasn't water, but air.

I was up where the birds flew – where they escaped from me to, when I chased them in our garden. I was conquering their world as well as mine. I was up, so far over the garden wall, I could go *anywhere*.

Now, this, *this* was adventure! This had to be why people went on them, to feel this way. Like they'd escaped their normal life, their normal world, even. To have no idea what happened next, but to be desperate to find out.

This window *wasn't* like any of the others, after all. Because this window was taking me somewhere new. Somewhere my days wouldn't just be measured in meals and naps and the same view from the same window. Somewhere I could discover who I was, outside of the house. Where I could be Lara the *outdoor* cat, the adventurous cat.

I was having the biggest adventure ever, and I was unstoppable.

It was enough to even make me forget Jennifer, and her vice-like grip on my stomach. For a moment, anyway.

Eventually the plane levelled out, and Jennifer's grip started to loosen. Freed, I shifted closer to the window, placing my paws against it as I looked out at the sky. The world looked incredibly big from here, like it might never end at all.

'Well, that doesn't get any better with practice,' Jennifer joked. Her forehead was beaded with sweat, her hands felt clammy.

'Are you okay?' Caitlin asked again, somewhat redundantly I felt, since Jennifer was clearly anything but okay. In truth, she was totally batty. Who wouldn't love flying?

Why on earth would Cleo give up the chance to experience all this? She said that she'd had enough adventures, but how could anyone ever get enough of feeling this way? I understood now why Gobi and Dad were always flying off somewhere new. There were so many places to go, too! I remembered the list Dad had given of places he'd been with Gobi, and all those pins in the map on the wall. Maybe, after Australia, I could fly to all of those places too!

Now I'd started, I never wanted to stop adventuring.

Jennifer was still breathing heavily, but she waved away Caitlin's question with a flap of her hand. 'Oh, I'll be fine,' she insisted, between pants. 'I usually am once we get going. At least, until the landing. But I have Cleo here to help me with that – don't I, Cleo?'

She nuzzled down into my fur, holding me tight against her again. I sighed, resigned to this sort of treatment for the rest of the journey.

But then Jennifer stopped, and held me out at arm's length – well, as much as the cramped airplane seating would allow.

'Cleo?'

I risked a look at her: she was frowning.

Oh. Drat!

I had a horrible feeling that the jig might be up. Cleo and I looked *almost* identical, but apparently, it was that *almost* that was about to get us caught.

Jennifer knew her own cat better, it seemed, than my humans knew me.

'What's the matter?' Caitlin asked. 'Is she ill? Or has she, you know, had an accident?' She pulled a face, and I gave her an indignant look.

Jennifer shook her head. 'Nothing like that. It's just …' she ruffled the fur at my neck to look for my collar: my bright pink with neon flowers on collar, to match my harness. The one normally completely hidden under my fluffy fur. But if a person knew to look for it …

I froze in her grasp. There was nowhere to run inside a plane. I could hide in any one of the small places I'd identified when I got on, but it didn't make any difference – they had a long, long flight to find me, after all. And then what? All the doors had been locked once we were all on board, and none of the windows even opened. I was trapped with Jennifer until we landed, at least.

Maybe she wouldn't find the collar. Or maybe it had fallen off somewhere, or something.

Or …

Hot, pudgy fingers gripped my collar, and pulled it a little way out from my neck, through my fur. I braced myself.

'This isn't my cat!' Jennifer declared, sounding outraged.

Oops. Busted!

Chapter
Five

'What on earth do you mean?' Caitlin asked. 'I thought you said she was your ESA?'

'She is!' Jennifer replied, indignant. 'At least, she *should* be. But this isn't my Cleo!'

I tried very hard to disappear back into my carrier, but Jennifer held on tight – tighter than she had even on take-off.

There was definitely no escaping now.

'How is that even possible?' Caitlin asked. 'Surely the security people checked her microchip and her pet passport? They don't just let *any* animals fly, you know.'

'I know! Believe me, she was Cleo when I put her in her carrier to get on the plane. But now, she isn't!'

'You know that's impossible, right?' Caitlin was looking at Jennifer like she was a crazy person. I actually felt a little sorry for Jennifer. I mean, she *was* pretty batty, but in this case, she was also totally correct.

'But it's happened.' Her eyes widened. 'Oh my word, if this isn't Cleo, how can I fly? How can I *land*?!' Jennifer's voice got louder with every word, and higher and shriller too.

I knew what that meant. It meant she was freaking out, like our neighbour in Edinburgh did when she found a spider in her house. (The first few times, they'd tried to get me to go round and eat it, except I have rather higher standards than that, thank you! After that, Mum or Dad went round with a glass and a piece of card that they somehow used to de-spider the house.)

I started to panic, too, as I realized how bad this could be.

If Jennifer freaked out and told the airplane people she'd brought the wrong cat on board, I had a feeling that things could go very wrong, very quickly. Why hadn't I thought about what would happen when Jennifer realized about the swap? It was all right for Cleo, safely back in the airport, waiting for someone to check her microchip and send her to a pet hotel. But what about *me*? Gobi had told me plenty of times how strict humans were about where and when animals could travel. There were all sorts of rules and regulations. What would they do to me when they realized I was on the wrong plane, or, worse, in the wrong country?

No, me freaking out, too, wasn't going to help anybody. I had to calm down.

I thought about blossom outside my window, floating on the breeze, and tried to slow my breathing down. Otherwise I was going to start panting like a dog, and that was just undignified.

The thought of engaging in dog-like behaviour was enough to distract me from my panic. And as my breathing slowed, so did my mind – enough to figure out what to do next, anyway.

I needed to calm Jennifer down too, I realized. Once she was calm, she'd figure out that she'd be in at least as much trouble as me if I was found out. Humans always blamed other humans for this sort of thing. They hadn't figured out that we animals could make our own decisions, thank you very much! She wouldn't want to get into trouble with the authorities either.

Once she realized that, she'd have no choice but to go along with the switch, right? Pretend that I was Cleo, too. It was the best option for both of us.

This could work. At least, it sounded better than throwing myself out of a window and hoping I could learn to fly really, really quickly, which was the only other plan I'd come up with.

So, step one: calm Jennifer down. Which, as an ESA for the day, was basically my job anyway. Hopefully, everyone would think she was just freaking out about the flight – that definitely wasn't a stretch of anybody's imagination.

I started with my best, most reassuring purr. The sort of deep vibration that settles human nerves on the basest of levels. It always worked for Mum when she was upset, anyway. It stopped Jennifer shouting, at least. Instead, she started panicking in a whisper, which was much better. Caitlin looked relieved about it, too.

Next, I nuzzled closer, right up under her chin, my soft fur swooshing over her skin like a really good stroke from someone who loves you. As I settled down against her stomach, still purr-ing, I lapped at her hand with my tongue, just enough to show her I cared. Then I butted my head up against her fingers until she started to pet me. It's hard for any human to be upset when they're stroking a cat as magnificent as me. Right?

Finally, Jennifer's breathing slowed back to its normal level, and I could no longer feel her heart thumping against her chest. Mission accomplished, I was the best ESA ever!

'So?' Caitlin asked, impatient. 'What *exactly* do you mean when you say Cleo isn't your cat? Is she acting funny or something?'

'I mean,' Jennifer said, in hushed tones, 'this isn't Cleo. This is a totally different cat. Look!' She tugged at my collar again. 'Cleo's collar is gold! Not whatever this is.'

Caitlin's eyes widened. 'But we already established that's not possible.'

Jennifer shook her head. 'Well, it's happened. I don't know how. It was definitely Cleo when I put her in the carrier, and now it isn't.'

To my feline mind, it was pretty obvious what had to have happened. But whether in her panicked state Jennifer had forgotten all about the other Ragdoll cat they'd met on the ferry, or – more likely, given what Cleo had told me about her – her instinct was simply to go for the more imaginative possibilities, she jumped to completely the wrong conclusion.

As I watched, her expression cleared, then brightened, and she made up her own explanation.

'You know, I think that maybe this was *meant* to happen,' she said.

Caitlin looked sceptical. 'Really? You were *meant* to lose your cat and accidentally end up with another one?'

'Oh, yes! I'm a firm believer in fate and destiny. Everything happens for a reason, you know,' Jennifer said, more confident in her theory with every word. 'So, this cat must have been sent to me for one, too.'

'You think the cat was *sent* to you? Why?' Caitlin's voice was heavy with disbelief.

'Well, that's the challenge, isn't it? To figure out the meaning behind the message. It's just like the time my purse was stolen in Barcelona, but on the way to the police station to report it, I found this glorious little piazza that I would never have seen otherwise.'

'Um, how is it like that?' Caitlin asked.

'Some things are just meant to be,' Jennifer explained. 'Even if we can't see the reason behind them when they happen. If you wait long enough, all will become clear.'

'Right. Just to make sure I've got this right,' Caitlin said. 'You honestly believe that the universe or whatever has sent you a replacement cat for some mystical reason that will become clear in time?'

Jennifer nodded excitedly. 'Exactly! Ooh, maybe she's here to guide me to the right place to scatter my Jeremy's ashes! After all, it's not like I've been having a lot of luck on my own.' Jennifer bounced a little in excitement at the idea. Caitlin just looked bemused.

I was with Caitlin on this one.

'Ashes?' she asked, faintly.

'Oh yes,' Jennifer replied, with an enthusiastic nod. 'That's why I'm taking this trip, you see. Well, that and to see my daughter, I suppose, although I'm not sure how keen *she* is on seeing me.'

'I see,' Caitlin said, in a tone that made it clear that she didn't see, not at all. Her hand was already inching towards the head-phones the flight attendant had given her. I decided she had to be a fairly optimistic person if she thought Jennifer was going to stop talking and let her watch a film any time soon.

Jennifer, I already knew, was a talker. She talked to anyone who would listen – including cats, if there were no humans around. I didn't mind a good conversation, but it did tend to be fairly one-sided between humans and animals. Still, I listened, because maybe she'd cast some light on the next stage of our adventure together.

'Before Jeremy went into hospital for the last time, I prom-ised him I'd find him the perfect place to spend eternity. He didn't want to just sit on the mantelpiece – he was an adven-turer, see. A traveller. I always put this down to his time in the Navy – you know, join the Navy and see the world and all that.'

'He was a sailor,' Caitlin said, obviously trying to find some thread in the conversation to hang onto.

'For years, until we settled down. But even then, we still travelled when we could. Used to be, flying was no bother at all to me, as long as I had Jeremy's hand to hold. But without him, I'm lost. That's why I need Cleo.' She squinted down at me. 'Or whoever this is. Anyway, what was I saying?'

'Ashes?' Caitlin said, faintly, clutching the headphones tightly.

'That's right! I promised Jeremy I'd find the perfect place to scatter his ashes. And I've been trying, ever since the funeral. But I'm still looking! I've tried Venice, where we went on our honeymoon; Rome, where we spent our fifth anniversary; Paris, where our daughter was conceived; Budapest, where we met some of our dearest friends on a river cruise; even Krakow, because I know he liked the salt mines there! But nothing ever felt quite right. Not the right vibe, you know? I'm a big believer in vibes, and instincts, and going with what feels right, so I meditated on it, and decided it was time to go further afield and spend some time with our family at the same time.'

'Just you and somebody else's cat,' Caitlin said faintly.

'Yes. Well, not intentionally, but that does seem to be the case.' Jennifer felt for my collar again. 'No tag, that's strange.'

I bristled. It wasn't strange, it was a personal choice – I never liked those metal things, and Dad had said that since I didn't leave the house, it didn't matter much anyway. Mum had sighed and put the tag away in the drawer, muttering about it being a good job I was microchipped.

Anyway, *my* choice. I wasn't judging her for her trust in crystals and vibes, was I?

(Actually, I was. But she didn't know that.)

'I really think that must be it. This beauty has been sent to help guide me to the right place to scatter Jeremy's ashes! It all makes sense.'

'Perfect sense,' Caitlin said, with heavy sarcasm.

But Jennifer didn't seem to notice. 'I guess that means it's up to me to name her,' she declared, delightedly.

'Are you sure it's even a *her*?' Caitlin asked, and I glared at her. *Of course* I'm female, couldn't she tell from my poise and grace?

'I'm definitely getting a female vibe,' Jennifer agreed, which might have been the first sensible thing she'd said since I met her.

She lifted me up to look into my eyes, and I stared back, willing her to somehow intuit that my name was Lara. Even if it meant she suddenly realized where I must have come from, and took steps to send me back to Mum and Dad. I could always escape again to continue my adventure.

My name was *my* name, I didn't want to be anyone except Lara.

'I think I'll name her "Fortune",' Jennifer said, and I sighed.

'Fortune is a terrible name,' I meowed to her, but she only beamed and said, 'I think she likes it!'

Another human with no understanding. Great!

And now I was stuck with her, searching for somewhere to scatter some ashes.

Jennifer snuggled me closer against her face. 'Oh, Fortune, I don't know how I'm going to cope without you on the next flight!'

Wait. What now?

I froze, listening intently, and hoping Jennifer would explain what she meant.

I thought the whole point of me being there was to fly *with* her. That was what an Emotional Support Animal *did*. And if I wasn't being squeezed almost in half on take-off, where would *I* be while she was flying? Cleo definitely hadn't mentioned this part.

'She can't fly with you all the way to Australia?' Caitlin asked.

Jennifer shook her head, oblivious to my confusion and distress. 'Australia will only allow in pets that travel in the hold, not in the cabin. I've got a two-night layover in America, because I wanted to catch up with a friend there, and the flights seemed to work best. Then, when we catch our next plane, poor Fortune will have to go back in her crate and get checked in again as freight, rather than a passenger. I've got it all arranged with the staff at the airport.'

Travel in the hold?! That wasn't the plan *at all*. Gobi had told me all about that when she flew across China in the hold of a plane, and it sounded *terrible*. She still had nightmares about it sometimes, even. Those nights, I had to wrap my tail even tighter over her.

Who would wrap their tail over me, afterwards?

Suddenly, Cleo's enthusiasm for swapping places for this trip made a lot more sense.

'That's a shame,' Caitlin said, which might have been the understatement of the century. But strangely, Jennifer wasn't looking too disappointed. Considering her distress at take-off, I hoped that meant she had a solution to all this: like not going to Australia after all, maybe.

'Actually, under the circumstances, this might all work out very well,' she said, looking down at me again, her gaze more assessing than adoring. 'The friend I'm staying with just happens to be a vet. One who might just be able to help me with "Cleo's" malfunctioning microchip in time for our flight to Australia.'

'Is her microchip malfunctioning?' Caitlin asked, frowning, which was what I wanted to ask too. As far as I knew, it had been working fine at the airport.

'It is now,' Jennifer said, decisively. 'America has some of the more relaxed pet import guidelines in the world, so getting Fortune in there as Cleo won't be a problem – I'll just tell them that the microchip has shifted and we can't find it under all that fur. Happens all the time with Ragdoll cats, I've heard. But Australia is a whole different matter.'

'They're pretty strict down under, huh?'

Hmm, I wasn't sure I liked the sound of 'strict'. Or vet friends, come to that. What *exactly* did Jennifer have planned for me? My previous visits to vets had rarely been any fun at all. I didn't want to start my adventure stuck in a vet's office, getting needles or something jabbed into me.

'*Very* strict,' Jennifer agreed. 'Multiple vet visits beforehand, paperwork to be signed and approved, and stringent checks on arrival. I'll need to have everything exactly in order to get her through – and I did, for *Cleo*.'

'But Fortune might need a little help from your vet friend,' Caitlin guessed, nodding. 'I get it now.'

'Australia's pet rules are one of the reasons I've put off going there for so long. Well, that and the quarantine,' Jennifer added, absently. A shiver ran through me, from my nose to the tip of my tail.

Quarantine?!

I knew about quarantine. Mum and Dad had talked about it a lot when they were trying to get Gobi home, after she'd been found. It meant being alone, locked up behind more windows, and not having any adventures at all.

I didn't want to travel in the hold of the plane, I didn't want to go into quarantine, and I *definitely* didn't want to be called Fortune. This was the worst adventure *ever*!

Meowing softly to myself, I settled down on Jennifer's lap, my tail wrapped around me and my paws under my chin, sulking. Suddenly, going back home to Mum and Dad didn't sound like a bad idea at all …

 # Gobi

China was almost like I remembered. Dion took me for a walk every day, and every day, people stopped to say hello and to make a fuss of me. We visited the canal we used to walk along when we lived in Beijing for a few months, before I was allowed into the UK. We stopped by the building where our old apartment had been, and he and Lucja drank coffee in the one Starbucks in the area that had allowed me in. In those ways, China was exactly like I remembered.

But last time I'd been here, with Dion, he was the only family I'd ever known. Well, Dion and Kiki and Chris, who helped do so much to find me, and to take care of me after I was found. Dion often said he'd have been lost without them — maybe even as lost as I'd been.

But when it was just the two of us, most of the time I was happy just to be there with him. And while I knew he missed Lucja, I was still new enough at this family thing not to realize what that really meant.

This time, I knew.

From the moment we all realized that Lara was gone — really gone — our family had been broken. It felt like I'd felt when my leg was injured, like we were limping along without all the parts needed to hold us upright and together.

I'd seen the distress on Lucja's face back in Paris as we huddled together, the three of us, waiting for our flight.

'What do we do?' she'd asked. 'Can we stay here and look for her?'

'We've looked,' Dion reminded her. And we had. Together, we'd scoured every inch of the airport, with no sign of Lara – or Cleo. 'But they're calling our flight now. We're just going to have to travel on without her,' he added, wrapping an arm around Lucja's shoulders. 'She's here in the airport somewhere, and they'll find her, I'm sure.'

'And what then?' Lucja had asked, voicing my concerns for me. 'What will happen to Lara then if we're not here?'

'I've already spoken with the airport staff,' Dion had reassured her. 'A lovely woman called Françoise promises me that as soon as they find her, they'll call and let us know, and that they'll keep her safe and happy here until we return.'

'I'm not sure I can go without her,' Lucja said, shaking her head. 'I know you need to get to China for the tour, but maybe I should stay here and keep looking for Lara.'

'We wanted to visit China together as a family,' Dion reminded her. 'And I know it doesn't feel right doing that when one of us is missing, but I trust Françoise. She's a cat lover, too – she showed me pictures of her four pets. She'll look after her. And realistically, the airport staff have more chance of finding her working together than you do on your own.'

'I suppose,' Lucja had replied, but her tone was grudging. 'But when they find her, I'm flying back and collecting her. It's true, this doesn't feel right without her.'

I agreed with Lucja: this was supposed to be our family holiday adventure, together, and now there were only three of us.

But the worst part – the part that kept me awake the whole flight to China, and most of that first night here – was that whichever cat Françoise found running around the airport, it wouldn't be Lara.

Lara was gone with Cleo's owner, Jennifer, and there was no way to be sure we'd ever see her again.

Once we were settled in Beijing, Dion called the Paris airport every day to find out if there was any sign of Lara yet. Sometimes he got to speak to Françoise, who would give him a detailed report of what she'd done and where she'd looked. Other days, if Françoise wasn't working, it would be one of her colleagues, who didn't give us nearly enough information.

Whoever Dion talked to, though, the bottom line was always the same.

There was no sign of Lara.

There was no sign of Cleo either, and I couldn't decide if that was a good thing or a bad thing. I hadn't given up hope that Lara might have managed to escape from the carrier too, and maybe she really would be discovered asleep in a pile of sweatshirts in the airport shop. But only Cleo knew for sure what had really happened.

Somehow, when they found her, I hoped I could be there to ask her the one question I needed to know the answer to more than anything.

Where was my sister?

It felt like for ever since I'd seen her. We carried on about our lives in China – making TV appearances and signing books in shops. Taking our daily walks and meeting new people.

And as time passed without her, I felt lonelier than I ever had before I had a family.

Dion and Lucja had almost given up hope of hearing from the airport, when finally, the call came. I saw the excitement and anticipation in their eyes, and was almost glad I couldn't tell them that it wouldn't be Lara. At least they still had hope.

'We've found a cat in Duty Free that matches the description of Lara,' Françoise said, on the speakerphone on Dion's mobile. 'Goodness only knows where she's been hiding all this time, or what she's been eating, but she looks healthy enough. I think she only came out because she got bored.'

'That certainly sounds like our Lara,' Dion said, relief colouring his voice.

But it wouldn't be Lara, I knew: it would be Cleo.

Françoise emailed over a photo, and we all huddled around the laptop, impatiently waiting for it to come through.

'It does look a lot like Lara,' Lucja said, tilting her head as she studied the picture.

'I don't know,' Dion said, doubtfully. 'It doesn't feel like her. Does that make sense?'

It did to me.

Maybe it was because I already knew it couldn't be Lara, because as much as the cat in the picture had the same fur, same colour eyes, same build as my sister, she still looked totally unfamiliar.

'Ask them to check the microchip,' Lucja suggested, and Dion nodded.

'I think they already are.'

It didn't take long for the answer to come through.

The cat wasn't Lara.

'I'm so sorry, Dion, Lucja,' Françoise said. 'I was so sure it was her, it looked just like the photos you gave me.'

'I know, I just don't understand. Where on earth is she?' Dion asked. I don't think he was really expecting an answer.

Which was just as well – nobody had one to give him.

I curled up on the hotel bed, put my head on my paws, and pretended that I could feel Lara's tail wrapping protectively around me. But I didn't sleep – I couldn't.

So, I listened instead.

'What do we do now?' Lucja asked. Dion placed his arm around her and pulled her close. 'I really thought Françoise would find her. I mean, how would Lara even get out? But what are the chances of there being two Ragdoll cats hiding in that airport?'

'Slim to none.' Dion sighed. 'She has to be somewhere, we just need to figure out where.'

'So, what? We go back and start searching the whole of Paris for cats?' I think Lucja was being what Lara calls 'sarcastic'. It didn't seem like a very good plan, anyway. 'You wouldn't even let me stay and search the airport.'

'No. You're right, we won't find her just walking the streets of the city alone. Besides, we're committed here in China for another week or so anyway.' Dion stood up and paced to the window, staring out at Beijing outside. 'But that doesn't mean we can't search Paris too.'

'I kind of think it does,' Lucja replied.

'No! Listen.' Dion spun around, excitement making his face glow. 'We found Gobi, right? Even though all the odds were against it, and there was no real reason to think we'd succeed.'

'Just like now, with Lara,' Lucja said slowly. 'So, you want to, what? Start a "Finding Lara" campaign? Like we did for Gobi?'

'Exactly! And we're in the perfect position to do it, too. Right in the middle of a tour, with the world's press listening and people paying attention. We can do this, Lucja, I know we can! We can find Lara.' He grabbed her hands, and she looked up into his face.

'I hope you're right,' she said.

So did I. Because it might be Lara's only chance of getting home.

Chapter
Six

I don't like to talk about what happened on our American layover. But needless to say, Jennifer's vet friend was a soft touch, had easy access to microchips and was happy to update Cleo's records accordingly. I wasn't sure it was at all legal, but Jennifer didn't seem too concerned about that. Apparently, she could 'sense' that I was in good health and no threat to the native population of Australia.

I was starting to understand why countries had animal immigration laws: it was because of people like Jennifer.

Still, her vet friend was also convinced of my good health (via rather more scientific methods) and seemed keen to help. I got the feeling she was rather worried about Jennifer. Which also made sense: Jennifer was a worrying person.

Anyway, eventually, I was fully registered as Jennifer's pet, Cleo, to match her passport, with a note about the new microchip. Hopefully, it would be enough to get me past the pet immigration controls in Australia.

'And if they have any concerns, at least they have the quarantine period to make sure she's in good health,' the vet said, smiling, as she handed me back to Jennifer.

I glared at her. And then at Jennifer too for good measure.

After a couple of days in America, Jennifer and I flew to Australia – her in the comfortable seats, me in my carrier in the cold of the plane's hold. I didn't much like being treated as freight – a thing, rather than a live, feeling animal. I consoled myself with the thought that this journey was all part of a bigger adventure. It would all be worthwhile once we reached Australia, and the real adventure began.

I curled up in my crate, tried to keep warm and attempted to sleep for as much of the flight as possible. It wasn't as much fun when I couldn't see the sky and the land below out of a window, but I dreamt of it instead, which helped. In my dreams, I was soaring through the skies, my paws and tail outstretched to help me glide on the breeze. A good – if a little chilly – dream, it kept me going until we landed.

I also don't like to talk about the 10 days I spent in quarantine in Melbourne, once the Australian border staff had been convinced that I was Cleo. Apparently, all animals flying into the country had to spend time in this one facility there, which meant I wasn't alone. Or special to anyone there.

I didn't like it.

Those 10 days, even more than my time with the vet friend, or the flight in the hold, were dark, dark times. Oh, the facility was comfortable, and we were fed regularly, but there wasn't the sort of love you get from a human you belonged to, and that was a loss. Even Jennifer made me feel important and loved. Here, I was just another animal, and the humans with me were just waiting to see if I developed any interesting diseases.

I spent most of my time there thinking about Gobi, and what she'd experienced in China, before Dad rescued her.

Maybe I'd been a little hard on her. Being locked up somewhere, away from your humans, that wasn't fun. And while I'd had Mum and Dad since I was a tiny kitten, Gobi had already lived a small life before she even found Dad. *What had that been like?* I wondered. It wasn't something she talked about at all, which made me think it was probably even worse than the flight in the hold, or the time she went missing. Which meant it must have been *really* awful.

I wondered how Gobi was coping, being back in China again, remembering what had happened last time she was there. For a moment, I wished I was there with her, for support. Then I reminded myself that Gobi had stolen my place as primary family pet, and that was why I was having this adventure to start with.

As usual, it was all Gobi's fault.

I wondered if Mum and Dad had noticed that Cleo wasn't me yet. Wondered if she had escaped, and if they'd all flown to China as a family of three.

Wondered if they were thinking of me, too.

At least at home, even if I stayed behind my windows, I had space to roam and explore. Space of my own, that I only had to share with Gobi – not every other animal that had flown into Australia in the last 10 days. The noises – the wails of sad, lonely pets who didn't understand why they were locked up there – kept me awake at night. And it goes without saying, there were no prawns to eat to make the whole experience even slightly less dreadful.

I don't think I've ever been as happy to see a human as I was to see Jennifer when she came to collect me after my quarantine.

That happy feeling didn't last long.

The windows in quarantine just looked out onto other rooms, not outside at all, so when Jennifer put my carrier on the passenger seat of the car she'd hired, and opened the door so I could peer out of the window, it was my first real sight of Australia.

To be honest, it didn't look all that much different to home, until we got outside the city.

We drove for what was possibly for ever – and would certainly have felt like longer if I hadn't just spent 10 days in a much worse place, and too many hours on planes before then. I couldn't wait to get to our destination, to settle in one place for a while. To discover the next stage of my big adventure.

Of course, that was before I met Jennifer's daughter.

We finally arrived in Sydney, after too much driving and quite a lot of stops for Jennifer to use the bathroom. It had been early morning when we left, but by the time we arrived, the sun was going down. I'd watched it trail across the wide skies, marking off another day spent away from my family. Another day waiting for my real adventure to start. Another day lost in transit.

The house we pulled up outside was lower to the ground than I was used to, like it didn't have any stairs inside. It was white on the outside, with blinds pulled halfway down each of the windows. There was plenty of space all around it. The front garden looked too neat for butterflies and other flying things to even risk visiting. The grass was too green to be real, and the few plants – in pots on stony gravel – had immaculately glossy green leaves but no flowers.

Just looking at it made me miss our garden back in Edinburgh. There was always something fun to chase there.

Jennifer rang the doorbell. Her face was set in an unfamiliar expression. Not quite a smile, or a frown. More blank, as if she were bracing herself for what came next.

As we were waiting for the door to open, she whispered to me without looking down. 'We might not mention that you're not actually my cat, Fortune. My daughter and son-in-law never met a rule they wouldn't follow blindly. They'll want you put back in quarantine, or worse – deported!'

I shuddered inside my carrier, and shrank back a little as the door opened.

I could tell instantly that the woman standing there was Jennifer's daughter. They had the same hair, same eyes, same mouth shape.

But apparently, the similarities ended there.

The daughter held herself rigidly upright, her bony shoulders straight and angular rather than Jennifer's plump, rounded ones. While Jennifer's eyes were creased with smile lines, her daughter's mouth had hard grooves beside it, as if it turned naturally down. While Jennifer's reddish hair was loose in a cloud around her heart-shaped face and pudgy cheeks, her daughter's hair was scraped back into a ponytail, displaying harsh, sharp cheekbones. But the biggest difference was in her eyes: they might have been the same colour and shape as her mother's, but while Jennifer's sparkled with laughter and excitement and adventure, her daughter's eyes were cold and flat.

I didn't like her. I wasn't even sure that *Jennifer* liked her, from the few things she'd said about her, and her expression waiting at the door.

'Mum! I can't believe you're really here at last.' I couldn't tell from her harsh, nasal voice if the daughter was pleased or not about that surprise.

'I told you I was coming!' Jennifer wrapped her arms around her daughter. 'Really, Kitty, what did you think? That I'd come all the way to Australia and *not* see you?'

Kitty … She'd called her daughter Kitty.

The woman really did have a thing about cats. Suddenly I had *slightly* more sympathy for Jennifer's daughter.

'Well, it *did* take you over a week to get here,' Kitty pointed out. 'We were expecting you *last* week.'

'I had to wait for Fortune to get out of quarantine!' Jennifer protested.

Kitty rolled her eyes. 'Of course you did.' Despite her mother's telling naming strategy, she clearly hadn't fully appreciated what was most important in Jennifer's life.

I couldn't disagree with Jennifer's priorities – obviously, cats were more important than people – but even *I* could see why Kitty might not like it.

'So, can we come in?' Jennifer lifted my carrier so Kitty could see in and study me the way I'd studied her. She didn't look impressed, or particularly pleased to meet me.

Not a cat person then. Obviously, I'd been right in my first impression of her after all.

'*Both* of you?' Kitty pulled a face. 'Really, Mum, you know John doesn't like pets. I thought …'

'And you know I can't fly without my cat with me! Not without your dad there. It's hard being an older woman on her own, you know. Thousands of miles away from her only family …'

Kitty sighed. 'Mum, you're getting carried away.'

Jennifer held my carrier aloft again. 'What do you want me to do? Leave her in the car? Look, Fortune's a perfect house guest, you'll hardly know she's here.'

Kitty didn't look convinced. I had to admit, this wasn't quite the reunion between a mother and daughter that I'd been expecting.

Shouldn't they be more pleased to see each other, at least? From what I'd gathered from Jennifer's rambling conversations, this was the first time she'd ever visited them in Australia. And the first time she'd seen any of them since Jeremy's funeral, over a year ago.

'Fine.' Kitty stood aside with a sigh. 'Just, *please*, Mum. Behave yourself while you're visiting?'

'I don't know what you mean,' Jennifer said, bristling.

'Yes, you do. This is *our* home, not yours, okay? So, none of that weird crystal hippy stuff while you're here. You know it just means that you and John get into arguments.'

'He has his beliefs, and I have mine. And neither of us are likely to change them for the other.'

Her head held high, Jennifer strode inside her daughter's house, leaving Kitty standing on the doorstep.

I had a feeling this might be an interesting visit.

Inside, Kitty's house was as white and sterile as the walls outside – no personality, no sense of home at all. White walls, white furniture, white rugs on white tiled floors. The only splash of colour came from a couple of pictures on the walls – not photographs, or pictures of people, just weird blobs of colour that didn't seem to mean anything. There was no map with pins here. No hint of adventure, or even anything personal at all.

I hated it all on sight, and resolved to shed as much fur on the furniture as possible, just to make it clear that someone lived there. Really, I was doing them a favour. Apparently, none of them knew what a home was supposed to look like.

As Jennifer carried me into the kitchen, two teenagers walked down the stairs. Not raced or jumped, or hopped or even stomped, just walked. Slowly, and without any enthusiasm at all. Clearly, they were as keen as their mother to see Jennifer – which was to say, not very.

'Look, kids, Grandma has come to visit!' To her credit, Kitty tried to sound excited.

The teenagers exchanged a look I couldn't read, then came forward in turn to hug their grandmother. Stiffly.

'Does Dad know she's here?' the boy asked.

'Not yet.' Kitty's smile turned brittle.

The girl rolled her eyes. '*That'll* be fun.'

Hmm. I didn't like the sound of that much, either.

Just then, the front door opened and closed again, quietly, deliberately. Whoever had come in didn't call out to say they were home, or try to find any members of their family, the way Mum and Dad always did. There were no animals scampering to meet the newcomer either, as Gobi and I liked to do. (Well, mostly Gobi – I usually waited to see if the visitor was worth my time first.)

When the new arrival appeared in the doorway I knew on sight this had to be Kitty's husband, John – and not just from the frown on his face.

You know how they say that people start to look like their pets, sometimes? In this case, Kitty had started to look like John, or maybe the other way around. And their kids weren't immune, either. It explained the strange sameness yet difference between Kitty and Jennifer, though. Maybe she'd once looked more like her mother, but years with John had started to transform her.

It was something in the straightened backs, the downturned mouths, and the disdainful glint in their eyes. I got a better look at the similarities as Jennifer let me out of my carrier, smiling at John the whole time. I'd bet money that he was the real cat-hater of the bunch – and that Jennifer was purposefully baiting him.

I made a mental note to always sleep on his chair. An act of solidarity with Jennifer, who'd brought me all this way on my adventure.

'Jennifer! You've come to visit. At last!' he said, crossing the room to hug her. At least, it looked sort of like a hug. He managed to keep a good cat's length between them, and patted her back rather than holding on. 'We were expecting you *last* week,' he added, exchanging a look with Kitty.

'Wild horses and excessive pet import rules couldn't keep me and Fortune away,' said Jennifer, gesturing towards me. 'Although they did delay us a bit, while Fortune was in quarantine.' I meowed a loud welcome, just to watch his mouth turn down a little further.

'Fortune? I thought your cat was called Cleo?' Kitty said, frowning in confusion. Everyone ignored her.

'My country just places a higher value on humans than animals, Jennifer,' said John.

I had a feeling they'd had this argument before.

'More fool them,' Jennifer replied. 'Now, where's Grandma's room, kids? Who wants to show me? Jack? Eleanor? I've got presents for whoever helps me with the bags!'

'Are they crystals?' the girl, Eleanor, asked.

'Good guess!' Jennifer clapped her hands together, gleefully.

The teenage girl tilted her head towards her brother. 'Jack will help you.' Then she disappeared back off up the stairs again.

Jack sighed. 'Come on then, Grandma. Your room is in the annex, next to the garage.'

'And the cat can stay in there too,' said John. 'Keep it out of the rest of the house.'

'Not on the bed though, please, Mum,' Kitty added. 'You know how I hate animals on the beds – the sheets never really seem to be clean again after a cat has slept on them.'

'Oh, I think you'll find that Fortune goes wherever she wants.' Jennifer shot me a knowing smile. 'She's quite an adventurer, this one.'

That was the plan, anyway. I just wasn't sure that this family could give me the sort of adventure I was looking for. They didn't seem like the adventurous type *at all*. Especially if pets on the bed were a step too far for them to be comfortable with. They were all so unlike Jennifer, it was hard to believe they even belonged to the same family.

That thought led me to thinking about my own family. I wondered what they were up to, over in China. And if they'd even noticed I'd gone.

Chapter
Seven

After spending less than a week with Jennifer's family, I knew for certain that this wasn't the adventure I was meant to be having.

I wasn't sure exactly what I'd expected from an adventure, before I'd left Edinburgh, but since then I'd had plenty of time to think about the subject. (Especially in quarantine. There was nothing much to do there *but* think.)

With so much time to think, I'd pieced together everything I knew about other people's adventures – Gobi's, Mum and Dad's, Cleo's, Jennifer's, even the late Jeremy's seafaring adventures. Everything any of them had ever said about adventures was added in and considered. So, by the time I'd been at Kitty's a week, I had a fully comprehensive checklist for my adventure – just like the lists Mum used whenever she was going shopping, or when we were packing to go to China.

My perfect adventure, I'd decided, needed the following elements:

1. Travel to new and exciting places – preferably places that Gobi has never been before.
2. See lots of new and exciting things – not through windows.
3. Meet new and exciting humans and animals – not cat-haters or pet immigration officials.
4. Get out and explore on my own – no humans or dogs allowed.

5. Have new experiences – ones I can tell Gobi about when I get home.

Number one, at least, I'd achieved, simply by flying into Australia. As for number two, while the first couple of weeks had been a bit of a failure on this part (unless you counted the interior of a plane or quarantine unit as new and exciting, and even then, surely it only counted for the first hour or two), since we'd arrived at Kitty's house, things were improving.

For number three, Jennifer herself, somewhat surprisingly, turned out to be good company – at least, when she wasn't on a plane. Ignoring her daughter's exasperated looks, and her son-in-law's not-so-quiet comments on her sanity, every morning she hooked me into a harness I presumed belonged to Cleo, and took me out to explore the city, looking for the right place to scatter Jeremy's ashes.

She'd made quite a project of it, listing everywhere she wanted to visit, and how to get there. But that was as far as the planning went. Finding the *right* place was a lot more complicated than picking somewhere out of the guidebook, it seemed.

'How will you even know what the perfect place is, Mum?' Kitty asked, one morning, as Jennifer collected her travel mug of coffee and waved goodbye. 'Can't you just go sightseeing like a normal person?'

'I'll just know,' Jennifer said, airily. 'Places have an aura, you know, Kitty.' Then she looked around the stark and empty house her daughter lived in. 'Well, *most* places do, anyway.'

She swept out of the door, me trotting along beside her, and headed into the city.

Actually, as far as I could tell, Jennifer *was* sightseeing. We explored all sorts of corners and interesting places in the city

– Jennifer helpfully reading from her guidebook to tell me all about them, too. I saw the Opera House, with its sweeping white roofs stark against the blue sky above and the water below.

'They call them "shells", you know,' Jennifer told me, as she sipped coffee at a cafe table outside the opera house one day. 'The roofs, I mean.'

I took a quick peek up, taking in the shells and the pinkish walls of the magnificent building, but to be honest, I tuned out when she started talking about all the exhibitions and concerts that had been held there. I was more concerned with how close we were sitting to the water: one false slip and I could be heading off the walkway and into the waves.

I inched back another few steps and waited patiently for our next adventure. Or even for Jennifer to decide *this* was the perfect place for Jeremy.

No such luck.

With a sigh, she put down her coffee cup. 'No, it's no good, Fortune. There's no vibe here. Come on, I want to try the Harbour Bridge next.'

A bridge. Over more water. Fantastic.

The Harbour Bridge wasn't the right place for Jeremy either, it seemed, although Jennifer and I were both very impressed with the views from the top. At least, I was as long as I didn't have to look down at the water below! (I was also very glad Jennifer didn't decide to walk the whole thing, as my paws were getting tired.)

Another day, we visited the Botanic Gardens.

'It's winter here, of course,' Jennifer said, looking around at dormant flower beds. 'I'm sure there's still plenty to see, though.'

And there was. Just not the perfect resting place for Jeremy.

We walked through lots of shopping streets, and stopped outside a large building Jennifer said was called the Queen Victoria Building. I wasn't allowed in most of the shops, but that didn't mean there still wasn't plenty to see.

Including a dog that talked human – well, almost.

'Look, Fortune!' Jennifer gasped, as we stopped beside a low, curved wall, outside the QVB. I looked up at her in confusion, until out of nowhere, I heard a voice.

'Hello, my name is Islay. I was once the companion and friend of the great Queen Victoria.'

I meowed in alarm, and Jennifer laughed, bending over to lift me up. She placed me on top of the curved wall, and I finally saw what had her so excited.

It was a small, dark statue of a dog – a scruffy sort of thing, really. Below it, enclosed by the curved wall, was a pool of water, filled with coins.

'Because of the many good deeds I have done for deaf and blind children I have been given the power of speech,' the voice continued. I looked closer at the statue. Obviously, it wasn't *actually* the dog talking, right?

'If you cast a coin into the wishing well now, I will say thank you.' As we watched, a tourist walked past and tossed a coin in.

'Thank you. Woof, woof!' Islay said.

'Isn't that brilliant?' Jennifer was already fumbling in her bag for coins to throw in. 'I bet you wish you could talk like Islay, don't you, Fortune?'

I glared at the statue; I got by perfectly well without having to steal words from humans. Making them understand you when you couldn't speak their language was the *real* achievement – that took far more talent, at least as far as I was concerned.

(I also felt totally vindicated later than evening, when Jennifer told her family about the 'delightful statue' and Eleanor replied that the real Islay had been killed after a fight with a cat.)

Another day, we took a day trip out in the car Jennifer had hired to a nature reserve to see kangaroos and other creatures in the wild. (I stayed in the car; there are some things definitely better observed from behind windows, however adventurous one might be.)

The point was, Jennifer explored every inch of each place we went. The woman checked *everywhere*. But nowhere seemed to satisfy her conditions for the final resting place for Jeremy's ashes.

I was starting to suspect that nowhere would. Maybe she just didn't want to let that last bit of him go, after all.

Anyway, back to me.

The point was, I was in a rut with Jennifer. Yes, I was seeing new and exciting things, but only from the end of my harness. I could only go where *she* wanted to go and see what *she* wanted to see. I wasn't free to meet new animals, or even new humans without her monopolizing the conversation. Kitty and her family were *definitely* cat-haters, so they didn't count towards my 'meeting exciting new people' rule, and the closest I'd got to meeting new animals was a statue of a *dog*.

Most of all, though, nothing new was happening. We were just *looking* at places and people and things together. If I wanted to look, I could have stayed home and watched the telly. I wanted to be involved, somehow.

Even if I couldn't quite put my paw on *how* yet.

One Saturday, Kitty declared they were all going to the beach, and meeting up with some of their friends. (Honestly, I was kind of surprised they had any.)

'Oh, Fortune will love that!' Jennifer clapped her hands together with joy at her (wildly inaccurate) statement. I know about beaches. They involve sand – which gets between my claws – and water. Not a natural cat environment. I mean, I know I said I wanted new experiences, but that doesn't mean I'd given up all my standards.

So, no, I didn't want to go to the beach, however much it might infuriate Jennifer's daughter to have me there.

I looked at Kitty. She was already glaring at me, hatred in her eyes.

'No,' she said. 'Mum, just *no*. We are *not* taking a cat to the beach. I've already had the neighbours asking about the lead and harness. And I can't even think about the state of the blankets on your bed. But most of all, I am *not* having you embarrass me in front of our friends by trying to get that cat into a swimsuit or something.'

Jennifer's eyes widened, as if she'd just been introduced to a whole new world of possibilities.

Yes, it was definitely time to get out of Kitty and John's house before Jennifer started dragging me to cat couture stores in the city, or something.

Fortunately for me, Jennifer lost the 'taking the cat to the beach' battle, but I'd hidden away behind the curtains on the lounge windows anyway, just in case. Kitty saw me, I knew, as the car pulled away out of the driveway – I could tell from the smug little smile on her lips, she thought she'd won.

Which meant that she thought Jennifer – and by extension, I – had lost.

Well, that was unacceptable.

I decided if I was going to leave, it was only right that I leave as many parting presents as I could for Kitty and John – besides, there wasn't much else to do in Kitty's house without anyone there to annoy.

First, I entertained myself by leaving fluffy fur over as many soft furnishings as possible, and walking over every kitchen surface. Then I took a nice long nap on Kitty and John's bed, rolling around in the sheets for maximum coverage.

I raided the kitchen cupboards for treats, but of course they had practically nothing in for me – only the pouches that Jennifer had brought for me, and I couldn't open them on my own.

I was getting impatient. Having made the decision to leave, I wanted to run immediately. But Kitty had also made sure all the windows were shut – and probably locked too. Not that my paws and claws could have opened them anyway.

So, I had to wait until night-time.

I wanted my escape to go as smoothly as possible, so I spent some time planning it, while I was free to roam about the house. My best bet, I decided, was the high window in the back hall-way, just outside Jennifer's room. It was closed at the moment, but I remembered that she always opened it before she went to bed, then left her bedroom door open a crack to let the breeze through.

It was perfect. As long as I could get up there and climb through …

I sat back on my haunches and stared up at the window. It was very high – and quite small, really.

Would I fit?

Checking over my shoulder to make sure the humans hadn't returned without me noticing, I cautiously jumped up onto the small hall table nearest the window. I really didn't want any witnesses to this, but a practice run definitely felt in order.

With a deep breath, I crouched down, then sprang forward and up, towards the window.

And came crashing down on the chair on the other side without even getting close.

Hmm … This was going to take some practice. I hopped down and headed back to the table.

Ten jumps later, I'd got close enough that I could check my whiskers would fit through. Whether the rest of me would be able to follow was something I couldn't figure out until the window was open, and I was ready to escape.

Tonight.

Eventually, much later that afternoon, the humans returned. On hearing the door, I dived back into Jennifer's room, curling up on the end of her bed as if I'd been snoozing the day away, while they were at the beach.

Jennifer bustled in to find me, of course, sweeping me up into her arms.

'Oh, Fortune, you would have loved the beach! The sand was gloriously white and the sea … oh, it went on for miles, the most beautiful azure blue!' She shook her head and sat on the edge of the bed with me on her lap. 'I felt for sure that Jeremy would love that place, but the pull I was waiting for, the sign that it was the *right* place to scatter him, it just didn't come.'

She sounded so disappointed, I brushed my head against her hand to comfort her, which had the added bonus of encouraging her to stroke me.

I really was starting to wonder if Jennifer would *ever* find the right place for Jeremy, even if she could bear to part with him. It seemed to me that there was only so much world, and if she hadn't found it yet, maybe she never would. Either way, I couldn't hang around here, waiting for her to discover it.

She thought I'd been sent to help her. But the truth was, I needed to get out and have my *own* adventure.

To my surprise, I found that I felt bad about leaving Jennifer alone with her family, especially after everything she'd done to take me with her to Australia. She could have left me to fend for myself in America, or even handed me in to the airport authorities. Who knew what would have happened to me then?

But I couldn't stay, either, for all that I was officially 'Fortune' and Jennifer's cat now. In my heart, I knew I'd always be Lara. And Lara had come all this way for an adventure – and I intended to find it.

That meant going it alone, just like Gobi had.

I waited until night fell, and everyone in the house had gone to bed – even Jack, who liked to stay up way too late on his computer (and would sometimes be persuaded to fetch me a snack, if I purred very sweetly). Once I was sure the house was totally silent, I crept on padded paws out of Jennifer's room and into the back hallway, where she had left that one small window slightly open, as always.

With a last glance back over my shoulder, I leapt up onto the table under the window, stared up at the opening and summoned all my courage: this was it. After all this time watching at windows, I was finally going *through* one.

I crouched down – and leapt into the unknown.

I'd like to be able to report that I made it through the window in one graceful swoop, like a cat-bird hybrid or something, but honesty compels me to admit that it wasn't *quite* so easy as that. However, with some scrabbling and clinging, and only a tiny bit of falling, I made it *outside*. Quickly, I scrambled out of the bush

I'd fallen into, round the side of the house and out into the street – where suddenly, the whole world opened up to me.

It was strange. I'd seen more of Outside in the last week than I had ever before in my life, but somehow this time it felt different. Maybe because of the darkness, and the strange noises that appeared from deep within it.

Or maybe because this time, for the very, very first time, I was alone. No harness, no human. Not even Gobi beside me to tell me how things worked in this Outside place.

Just me. Lara.

And a really big adventure, just waiting for me to find it.

I sniffed the air – cool with night breezes – put one paw on the pavement before me, and strolled away from Jennifer, the house, and everything that was even a tiny bit familiar.

The world felt big. But right then, I felt bigger.

I felt *free*.

 Gobi

It was like Dion and Lucja had been taken over by excitable puppies or something. Gone were the forlorn and hopeless humans they'd become over the last couple of weeks in China. In their place were motivated, determined people, totally certain that they would find Lara in Paris.

I had no way of explaining to them that I didn't think Lara was in Paris any more. But still, their hope was infectious, and I found myself making up stories of how she might have escaped and stayed in France, exploring the city and making friends. In my stories, she was always happy and safe – I couldn't bear to imagine anything else.

'What about this one?' Dion pointed to a photo of Lara on the computer screen. They were trying to find the best image to use for their new campaign.

Lucja pulled a face. 'I don't know, it doesn't really show off her colouring well.'

'You're right.' Dion scrolled down through the photos on the screen. 'This one better?'

'Much.' Lucja nodded. 'That looks like Lara.'

I padded over and peered up at the screen. In the photo, Lara was scowling, her head held high and her fluffy tail swished around her side. Just like I remembered her.

Spotting me, Dion reached down and pulled me up onto his lap. 'You miss your sister, don't you, Gobi?'

I barked in agreement, making them both laugh – it was nice to hear them laugh again.

'Don't worry, we're going to find her. We're going to make this photo go viral, until anyone who sees her can't help but know she belongs to us. Just like when we found you.'

His voice was full of confidence – so full, I almost believed him. But I couldn't help but think there were differences. When I'd been missing, at least they'd known what country I was in. And most importantly, I'd wanted to be found.

But the more I thought over that day in the airport, picturing events in my head, the more I started to wonder.

Lara hadn't made any fuss when she was picked up and put in the wrong carrier. And she always let people know when she was unhappy. So why hadn't she?

The only thing I could think was that she had run away on purpose. But why? And did that mean she didn't want to come home at all?

I was still contemplating the possibilities when Dion looked at his watch and declared we were going to be late for the next TV interview. I'd been in a lot of TV studios since I came home with him. After he found me, everyone wanted to hear the full story – especially all the people who'd donated to help bring me home. So, Dion would take me around to do interviews and talk about our adventures, so everyone could see that I was happy and healthy now. I quite liked it – there were lots of lights and new people and interesting smells, and someone would usually find me something exciting to eat, too.

Today's trip to the studio was a lot more important, though. Today, as much as the TV people might want to ask questions about the new book, Dion and I had something much more important to talk about.

Lara.

'How does it feel to have the whole world read about your adventures with Gobi?' the interviewer asked.

Dion turned to the camera to answer. He'd been asking questions before they started filming about translations and subtitles. I didn't know exactly what they were, but I knew that he was making sure that everyone who watched this would understand what he was asking them.

'I'm so happy to share Gobi's story with our readers all over the globe,' he said. 'But today, what I'd really like to talk about is what happened next. Because the next part of the story is sort of about Gobi, but it's also really about her sister – Lara the Runaway Cat.'

And then he was away, telling the whole story of everything that had happened since that airport in Paris.

Soon, the whole world would be looking for Lara.

I just hoped they could find her.

Just a few days later, our trip to China was over. I'd spent so long being nervous about returning there, then looking forward to being there together as a family, that the actual trip – without Lara – went by in a blur of missing my sister and trying to find a way to get her back.

Dion's interview had kicked off a viral online campaign that saw hundreds of thousands of people sharing photos of Lara online. This time, he said, things were different: they weren't trying to raise money, just awareness. They wanted every person on the planet looking out for Lara – and to contact us if they saw her.

So far, no one had. But it was only a matter of time, Dion said.

I hoped he was right. But the campaign was focussing on France, first and foremost. And I just knew that Lara was no longer there.

Still, as we travelled back to the UK through the airport in Paris where I'd last seen my sister, I couldn't help but scan the hallways and terminals for her. I realized after a moment that Dion and Lucja were doing the same. As if, even after weeks, we all expected her to stroll casually out of one of the shops and say, 'Oh, you're back, are you? Didn't fancy China myself, so I decided to stay here.'

I'd have given every last dog biscuit I had for that to happen. But it didn't.

And so we headed for the car, then the ferry home, and then the long drive back to Edinburgh. Where I knew I'd only find more reminders of my missing sister.

But Dion had more TV interviews, podcast appearances and Internet events planned. He told Lucja that he wouldn't stop until he'd covered every sort of media, social or otherwise.

He would bring Lara home.

Chapter
Eight

That fantastic feeling of freedom lasted me all through that first night as I prowled the streets searching for adventure, taking in all the sights and the sounds of the city. Or actually the suburbs, I suppose. That was what Jennifer had called them, when we'd been travelling into the city proper together. The city centre was a whole train ride away.

But for now, exploring the suburbs was adventure enough for me.

Everything sounded different to Edinburgh – or maybe I'd just never heard a city sound this way from behind my windows. But the smells were different too. I spent many happy hours chasing down a scent, finding interesting things in back alleys and gardens.

The houses were more spread out than back at home, and lower down too. I'd never explored Edinburgh at night like this, but I'd watched it through my window, and through the windows of the car once when we were driving somewhere, late, after dark. Edinburgh had lots more tall buildings, and lights everywhere – on lamp posts or behind curtains. Here, the lights felt more scattered and there were large patches of dark between them for a cat to hide in.

There were people around still, too, for a while. I watched them going about their lives – free from harnesses or needing someone else to take them places. I was just like them now, too, I realized.

I could go anywhere, do anything.

And I would.

The freedom euphoria wore off around breakfast time, when my stomach growled and I realized some terrible truths about adventures. Yes, I was alone and free, but that freedom came at a cost.

Alone, I had nobody to feed me. To stroke and pet me. To look after me.

Where, for instance, did a cat get prawns in the suburbs, without a human to supply them? Even those pouches of food that Jennifer insisted on feeding me were better than nothing – and even they were beyond my ability to find and eat alone.

I'd spent so much time and energy focussing on my escape, on getting out into the world to have my own adventure, I hadn't stopped to think about how it would work once I got there.

By this time, I'd walked an awfully long way from Kitty's house. I could probably find my way back there if I needed to – my own trail was still fresh, after all. But that felt too much like giving up, far too soon.

Taking a moment to sit on a wall, watching the sun rise, I reminded myself of the rules I'd set for my adventure, and how I couldn't fulfil them with Jennifer. Going back would be turning my back on *true* adventure. Gobi hadn't had anyone to feed her, once, either – before she found Dad – and Gobi had survived, she'd made it on her own. And that meant I could too.

I had to go on. And that meant finding a way to feed myself.

Some cats, I knew from conversations at the vet's, or with Gobi, were mousers – kept to catch mice and eat them. Others chased birds, for sport and for food. (Actually, *I* chased birds in our little back garden in Edinburgh. But apparently, other cats actually *caught* them, which seemed to be the crucial difference.) Some, and I shuddered a little at this, ate spiders, like our neighbour in Edinburgh kept hoping I would.

The common thread was that they all caught their own food.

I wondered where a cat had to go to catch a prawn – maybe a supermarket? That was where Dion and Lucja seemed to go for *their* food.

I'd walked far enough to be past the houses and coming into a small shopping area – not one of the big city ones that Jennifer and I had explored, but hopefully, big enough to provide me with some breakfast. Now the sun was up, humans were starting to be out and about, too, bustling about their days as humans did, without paying much attention to wandering cats, or the exciting smells and sounds of their city.

Humans always knew where the food was, so they could lead me to it, I hoped.

I followed one purposeful-looking human to a large shop with bright strip lighting. The doors opened for her automati-cally (something that had surprised and confused me the first time I'd seen it happen, at the airport), so I trotted in behind her. Maybe she'd spot me and toss me a prawn, or even a dog biscuit. (I was so hungry, I couldn't really afford to be picky, and maybe this would be the one time I wouldn't be sick after eating it.)

In fact, I could see shelves of packets with cats on the front, just there in the aisle in front of me. I wasn't a big fan of packaged cat food, but it was definitely better than nothing. If the woman shopper could just open the corner of one for me …

But she barely seemed to notice me at all as she picked up her basket and started wandering around the aisles. Unfortunately, the shopkeeper did.

'Out! No cats in my shop, how many times do I have to tell you? I might not be able to keep you lot from ravaging my bins out back, but I can definitely keep you out of here! Now, shoo!' He swept me out of the automatic doors with his hands and I scarpered as told.

Then I sat outside the shop and thought. Hard.

He couldn't *keep* me out, right? It was a shop. Open to the public. All I had to do was walk up to those doors and they'd open for me again. I'd just need to be a bit sneakier and make sure he didn't see me. Then I could try and grab one of those bags of food and run out with it. I was sure I could figure out a way to open it with my teeth and claws eventually.

But when I approached the automatic doors, nothing happened. I wiggled around a bit to show them I was there, but still, they didn't open.

On the other side of the glass, I could see the shopkeeper glaring at me.

This wasn't going to work.

'Don't you know those doors only work for humans?' A large, ginger Tom prowled across the pavement behind me, heading around the corner of the shop. 'Us cats have to get our food another way.'

I stared at the doors again. How did they know? Were they really so clever that they could tell the difference between cats and humans? And what about dogs? I bet they let *dogs* in – the world was so clearly biased towards dogs.

Gobi would have been able to get in, I was certain. But I definitely couldn't.

With a last, mournful look at the food shop, I followed the Tom around the corner to ask his advice on catching things to eat. Preferably prawns. Cats helped other cats, right? I mean, I hadn't met many other cats beside Cleo, but the Tom seemed to know how things worked around here, so I was sure he'd want to help me if he could.

But when I reached the alleyway behind the shop, I realized the Tom hadn't been alone. Five cats ranged around the alleyway, perched on top of large containers full of rubbish, or on the doorstep from the back of the shop, or even a low roof belonging to the building behind. One of them was missing an eye, another half its tail. They all looked unkempt and uncared for. And they were all staring right at me.

In all the time since I'd left home, I'd never felt more out of place than I did right then. My fur was still fluffy and glossy, my tail intact, my eyes clear and blue.

I didn't belong here. But in that moment, I had nowhere else to go.

'Found this one trying to get through the doors,' the Tom said. 'Think she wanted to go shopping like a *human*.'

The cats all laughed, high and cruel. I felt the sound in my chest, and it made me want to run. But where? These cats – distasteful as they were – were my best chance of finding something to eat. Even if they didn't look like they'd ever even *tasted* a prawn.

I bet they lived on spiders. Urgh!

'I was just looking for something to eat,' I said, as neutrally as possible. I couldn't risk being friendly yet, but I didn't want to offend them, either. 'Perhaps you can help me?' Pushing it, maybe, but I really *was* starving.

The cats laughed again. 'Looking for food?' the one-eyed cat said. 'Aren't we all?'

'So, where do you find *your* food then?' I asked. While none of the cats were plump, they didn't look exactly malnourished, so they had to be eating something, right? Something more than just spiders. I had to swallow my pride and learn from them if I wanted to survive out here alone.

'Here.' Another cat dived into the rubbish as she answered. 'And there,' she added, reappearing with half a sandwich in her mouth.

Maybe it was a *prawn* sandwich. My mouth started to water at the idea.

Then I caught myself.

Eating rubbish? Was this what I'd come to?

The cat wolfed down the sandwich, and I admitted to myself that yes, this was *exactly* what I'd come to, if it meant I got some breakfast.

'Great,' I said, with more enthusiasm than I really felt. 'Thank you.'

I hopped up onto the edge of the rubbish bin, eyeing the waste below and preparing to dive in, when suddenly the Tom was on the ledge beside me, his claws out.

'Not so fast,' he said, one paw right next to mine, close enough to wound if he chose.

I froze. 'But she said …'

'She said that this is where *we* get *our* food,' the Tom interrupted. 'But you're not one of us, are you?'

'What do you mean?'

I was a cat, wasn't I? Wasn't that good enough?

Cats helped other cats, didn't they?

Apparently not.

'I can tell you're not from around here. Not with that accent. And your pampered princess act. Looking for *humans* to feed you?' He shook his head. 'That's not how we do things, Princess.'

'My name is Lara,' I corrected him. 'And it's not how *I* do things any more, either.'

'So, you think you can just waltz in here and start eating our food, is that it?' One-eye had come up behind me while I was focussed on Tom. I spun round, almost losing my balance on the ledge, which made all the cats laugh. Embarrassment flooded through me at the sound.

I had to prove that I was every bit as good as these cats; that I could make it on my own, too. If they thought I didn't need their help, maybe they'd offer it, contrary as that seemed to me.

'I … I thought you were offering to share.' Even *Gobi* shared her food with me sometimes, although it did tend to make me ill. Goodness only knew what food from the bin would do to my poor stomach.

'You thought wrong.' The cat with the sandwich landed on the ledge across from me. I glanced behind me, and found the other two cats waiting on the ground.

I was surrounded.

'Okay, look, I'll just go now.' I tried to take a few steps, but One-eye was waiting one way, and Tom the other. There was nowhere for me to go but down – either to the cats on the ground, or into the bin.

At least the bin had food in it, this might not be all bad.

Into the bin, or onto the ground and running away? Which way should I jump?

I needed to show them I wasn't scared by their threatening tactics – even if I was. They needed to know they couldn't intimidate me, or scare me away – not when breakfast was at stake, anyway.

There was a pause – a silent, heavy one – while we all waited to see what the other side would do.

In that moment, I made up my mind: this wasn't just about breakfast, this was about the kind of adventure I wanted to have. The sort of cat I was now.

I wasn't running anywhere.

I didn't give them any warning, I just lurched sideways into the bin and flailed around in the rubbish, looking for the other half of that sandwich. One-eye screeched and jumped in after me, followed by his friends, and soon we were all in there, scratching and fighting to get the best bits. I yowled as someone's claws caught my side, and another cat let out a howl as I caught their tail with my teeth, when it got between me and some food.

The noise must have been tremendous – we cats certainly aren't quiet when we fight, it turns out – because before I knew what was happening, the shopkeeper was there again, shouting at us, hauling us out by the scruffs of our necks and tossing us down into the alley again.

'All of you, get out of here!' he yelled, his broad face bright red with anger.

The other cats yowled, and turned away. I started to follow them, but a few hisses made it clear that was a bad idea. I hung back, the shopkeeper still glaring at me.

Where did I go now? The alley cats might not have been friendly, but they were at least *cats*. If I couldn't rely on humans *or* cats, what was I supposed to do now?

'You'd better be gone before I come back with the bins,' the shopkeeper muttered, turning away.

He slammed the back door behind him as he went back into the shop. I took another few steps towards the edge of the alley, wondering if it might just be worth another look for that half a sandwich …

Suddenly I realized I wasn't alone in the alley at all. There was another human there, a young girl, who was looking at me and shaking her head. She had light brown hair, plaited back away from her face, and kind hazel eyes that told me I needn't be afraid of her.

I liked her on sight.

'You didn't belong with those angry cats, anyway.' She crouched down beside me, watching me carefully, and suddenly I realized what an awful picture I must make. My fur was matted with dirt, and damp from whatever had been leaking in the rubbish bin (I didn't like to ask), and one of the cats had scratched my side so it stung. I definitely didn't look like the princess cat the Tom had accused me of being. Plus, I was so hungry, I could cry.

I never did find that half a sandwich …

I let out a pitiful little whine, and the girl tentatively patted my head, presumably on the only clean patch I had left.

'I'm Anya,' she said, softly, as she stroked between my ears. 'Would you like to come home with me? I can clean you up and find you some food. I think there's still some left from before … before Dad had to take Millie into the vet's and she didn't come home again.' Her eyes turned sad as she said the last bit, and looking at her, I saw the same sort of loss I saw in Jennifer's eyes, sometimes.

Now her kindness made sense: she was mourning her own lost cat. I felt very sorry for her, which, given that *I* was the one who'd been attacked and covered in rubbish, seemed strange. But another part of me couldn't help but think if Anya's cat was gone, and no one was eating her food, it would be a shame for it to go to waste, right? Besides, Anya looked like she needed some company. And right now, to me humans definitely seemed like a better option than other cats.

I gave an enthusiastic meow and Anya understood me instantly. Standing up, she motioned for me to follow her and, without hesitation, I did.

This adventuring alone thing was overrated, anyway.

Maybe the people I got to meet on the way could be *part* of my big adventure.

Chapter
Nine

Anya's house wasn't too far away from the shop where she'd found me. I trailed along behind her, along streets and across roads. She always waited for me before crossing, as if I couldn't make sure it was safe on my own. (Which, in fairness, might not have been totally wrong. It wasn't like I'd had to cross a lot of roads alone in my life. Even since leaving Jennifer's daughter's house I'd mostly just stuck to one side as far as possible.)

'I can't take you inside, I'm afraid,' she said, as we reached a single-storey home that didn't look very different to Kitty's from the outside. My heart started to sink: was I going to be as unwelcome here as I had been with Jennifer's family? 'My mum would be cross. I think she was actually glad when Millie died, you know. But don't worry, I've got somewhere you can stay out back. Come on!'

I followed her around the side of the house, into the back garden. This, at least, looked nothing like the carefully mani-cured lawn, artistically pruned shrubbery and paved patio at Kitty's house. Instead, there were plants growing wild with a riot of coloured flowers, and a row of trees at the far end of the garden. It wasn't anything like our small garden back at home in Edinburgh, really, but somehow it *felt* more like home.

Like somewhere I could belong.

Ignoring all the flowers and the thick grass for pouncing in, Anya headed straight for the trees, so I went too, resisting the urge to chase after butterflies or dandelion fluffs.

'It's just up here,' she said, as she reached the row of trees. Many of them had lost their leaves for the winter, but there were a couple of evergreens and ferns – like the houseplants we had at home, but lots bigger – growing underneath them. I was already imagining all the places I could hide and explore in this garden when, without warning, Anya shot up the trunk of the nearest tree and disappeared!

I sat at the bottom and stared up after her. Had the tree eaten her? Did it plan to eat me too? I'd never met a cat-eating plant before, but maybe they were particular to Australia, rather than Edinburgh.

'Come on!' Anya's face appeared between the mostly bare but still thick branches, grinning down at me. 'You're a cat. Haven't you ever climbed a tree before?'

I had no way to tell her that, actually, no, I hadn't ever climbed a tree. I'd never had any reason to. There weren't any in our little garden in Edinburgh, or many by the side of the motorway when we stopped to stretch our legs on car trips. And even if there were, what could possibly be up a tree to make me want to climb it?

But now I had a reason: Anya had cat food. So, if she wanted me to climb a tree …

I stuck out a tentative paw, and tried to grip onto the tree bark with my claws. It seemed to work …

It took a few tries, and some undignified grabs for low-hanging branches, but eventually, I made it far enough up the tree trunk for Anya to reach down and scoop me up, laughing as she did so.

'You know, I really don't think you *have* ever climbed a tree, Puss, have you?' She started to cuddle me close, before obviously remembering the state of my fur after the rubbish bin. 'Come on, let me show you my tree house.'

A tree house, it turns out, is exactly what it sounds like – a house in a tree. This one was quite small, but it had a door, two windows with plastic over them, a single chair, and a few cushions on the floor. She placed me on one of the cushions and studied me, carefully.

'You're not going to like this, Puss, but you're going to need a wash. And a comb. Trust me, it's for the best.'

She was right – I didn't like it.

The problem with having such luscious, fluffy fur is that it does take some looking after. Back at home, Mum and Dad used to argue about whose turn it was to try and brush me. You see, even though I *know* my fur needs brushing to keep the knots at bay, that doesn't mean I actually enjoy it. I can usually take it for a few minutes – which is about long enough for them to do a small segment of my luxurious fur – but after that, I'm done.

And of course I need to let them know when I've had enough – which I usually do with my claws.

I guess I can understand why they don't like brushing me. (And don't get me started about when they decide it's time to trim my claws and fur. That is simply *not* okay, whatever they say about it preventing me from ripping up the cushions or coating the whole floor in cat hair.)

Anya lowered herself back through the doorway, leaving me in the little tree house. I padded to the door to watch her go. She seemed to be using some sort of wooden and rope ladder thing – I wondered if that was easier than scrambling up the trunk.

'And I'll bring food, too!' Anya called up, as she jumped to the ground.

Well, in that case, I supposed I could take a bit of brushing. Even I had to admit that I needed it right now – I knew from bitter past experience that avoiding a brush for too long only led to knots in my fur that pulled at my skin. It was worth it anyway to stop my stomach from rumbling.

Besides, I still didn't actually know how to climb *down* from a tree.

Anya returned a while later, carrying a large rucksack she told me was full of supplies.

'We've got water,' she said, pulling out a large plastic bottle and placing it on the floor. 'Some soap, a flannel and a sponge, one of Mum's old combs, a towel to dry you off, Millie's old cat bed for you to sleep in, a bowl for food and another for water, and … cat food!' She pulled the pouch out with a flourish, and my stomach growled.

It was almost hard to remember that I'd once turned my nose up at any sort of food that came in a tin or a packet. Compared to the half a sandwich from a bin I'd been contemplating for breakfast, this was the height of luxury.

Anya laughed at the sounds from my stomach. 'Was that you? I guess I'd better feed you before I try to clean you, then.'

Sensible girl. I definitely wasn't going to be able to keep my cool while being brushed if I hadn't had something to eat first.

She ripped open the pouch and transferred the contents to one of the bowls, carefully filling the other with water. I barely waited for her to move away before I dove in. I swear, packet food has never tasted so good as it did in that tree house!

The cleaning and brushing part was less fun, but a full stomach made it just about bearable. Anya talked to me all the way through, so I focussed on her voice, rather than the tug and pull of the comb. There were only a couple of times when I got fed up and my claws came out, but Anya calmed me and reminded me that I didn't want to smell this bad for ever, so she had to clean me.

I acquiesced, with moderately good grace.

Just remind me never to fall into a giant bin again, okay?

'It'll be nice having you here to stay,' Anya said, as she sponged me down. 'It's been kind of lonely here since Millie died. I mean, she was the only one who used to really listen to me. I don't really have so many other friends at school, you see. Or any, actually.'

She sighed, and I butted my (now clean) head up against her hand in sympathy. I understood being alone, now. And while before, I'd have thought it to be a good thing – especially if it meant not having to share my humans and my prawns with Gobi – I knew now how hard it could be.

I missed Mum and Dad every day – even when I was with Jennifer, having adventures. I'd thought the ache would go away, but it seemed to only get bigger, the further away I was and the longer we were apart.

'I used to have a friend,' Anya went on, as she continued wetting, soaping, rinsing and combing my fur. 'My best friend, Dawn. We'd been friends since we started school. We did everything together – we were in the same class, the same clubs, we liked the same things. I didn't need any other friends while I had Dawn. But then Dawn's dad got this job hundreds of miles away, in a whole different city, so they moved. So, then it was just me and Millie. And now it's just me.'

She sounded so lonely, it made my heart bleed for her.

How had Gobi coped with it, I wondered, all that time she was separated from Dad in China? Back home, she always wanted to be with people – curling up with Mum or Dad on the sofa, or wriggling her way into my bed at night. She was always ready to accompany anyone anywhere, as if she just didn't want to be left alone.

I liked being alone sometimes, but even I had to admit, I was glad when Mum and Dad came home again. And Gobi too, mostly.

My mind drifted to Gobi, and China, and how my family was coping without me. Was Gobi lonely, without me there for company? Was she scared, to be back in China again? Did she miss me, the way Anya missed her cat, and her best friend?

I shook my head – I was too busy adventuring to think those thoughts now.

Instead, I turned my full attention back to Anya, who sighed, and reached for the comb.

'So, yeah, it's just me,' she continued. 'And school, it's not my favourite place these days. I dread Mondays – tomorrow is Monday, in case you cats don't keep track of the days of the week.' I didn't, so this was useful information. 'The other kids at school … it was okay when Dawn was there, because we looked after each other. But now it's just me, they think I'm an easy target. The other girls say I'm not one of them, because I don't like the same things they do. Because I'd rather be up in a tree house than shopping for clothes or whatever.'

That sounded like the sort of things the alley cats had been saying to me: that I didn't fit in, because I was too much of a princess. And apparently, my new friend wasn't enough of one for the other girls at her school. But who wanted clothes over tree houses? Tree houses had cushions and food and places to curl up and nap. Clothes – I know, from Mum and Dad's one attempt to get me into some sort of cat coat one very cold winter when I wanted to play in the garden – just squash your fur and rub in uncomfortable places. Tree houses were *clearly* superior. And therefore, so was Anya, whatever those other girls might have said.

I rested my head against Anya's leg in solidarity. Maybe we weren't like other cats and people. But maybe that was just because we were much, much better. I definitely liked Anya more than I'd liked any other humans for a while. At least since yesterday, anyway.

That made me think about Jennifer, for the first time since I'd escaped Kitty's house. While I might not be sure how my family were coping in my absence, I could guess exactly how she was reacting to my disappearance.

She'd thought I was sent there to help her. The fact that I'd gone away again wouldn't have fitted well with her quest to find the right place for Jeremy's ashes. The thought made me feel uncomfortable. I hadn't wanted to upset Jennifer, but I couldn't have the adventure I needed with her. Did that make me a bad cat, for running out on her, after everything she'd done for me? No, I decided. A cat had to look out for herself first. I just wished – not for the first time – that I was able to talk to humans better. That I could have explained to Jennifer why I was leaving, maybe even made plans to come back again, one day. As it was, she'd never be sure what had happened to me.

Maybe she'd just assume the same forces that had brought me into her life had taken me away again, off to help some other human instead. After all, I'd done my best to help her, hadn't I? I'd toured most of Sydney with her. It wasn't my fault the auras and vibes and what have you weren't talking to her the way she'd hoped.

Jennifer would be fine, I reassured myself. Just like Gobi and Cleo, and Mum and Dad would be. They were all having their own adventures, and I was having mine. That was all.

That night, I slept in Anya's tree house alone, wrapped up in a blanket she'd brought me, full of (inferior, but satisfactory) food, feeling safe and warm. Maybe it wasn't *exactly* what I'd imagined when I'd thought about my adventure. But then here, on the other side of the world, separated from my family, cared for by people who didn't even know my name … I couldn't even remember what I'd imagined an adventure would be like. Safe back home in Edinburgh, I'd only thought about getting on the other side of those windows. Seeing the real world. Proving that I could do anything that Gobi could.

I'd done that – I'd escaped, I'd run away on a plane, I'd even changed my name. I'd discovered a whole world I never knew existed, beyond a map on the wall and some shiny silver pins. But now I was here, I had a feeling that I had a lot more to learn about the real world before my adventure would be done. But I'd gone new places. I'd explored alone, without a harness. And I'd met new people.

Like Anya.

She was a sweet girl, I decided, remembering the gentle way she'd washed and combed me, careful of my scratches and sore spots. She didn't deserve to be as sad as she was, without her friend or her cat. She'd saved me – from the alley cats, the shopkeeper, starvation, loneliness, not to mention smelling like a bin for the rest of my days. Maybe I could save her in return. Or help her, at least.

She was mourning the loss of her cat, of course. And while I couldn't take Millie's place, or stay and be Anya's new pet for ever, maybe I could help ease that transition. Be company for her until she was ready to move on – the way Cleo had been company for Jennifer after her husband died. That was easy enough, and it meant regular food and shelter for me, too. A

win for everybody. As for the best friend who moved away …
Maybe Anya needed to find a new best friend, someone else to
share her tree house and her worries with.

Maybe that was something else I could help her with, before
I moved on again.

I just wasn't sure how, yet. But I was sure it would come to
me.

I mean, I was basically a genius cat. After all, I'd made it all
the way to Australia on my own. (Okay, with a little bit of help,
if you're being picky.) Surely, I could find a little girl a new
friend somehow, right? I just had to wait for inspiration to
strike. And enjoy the food and the cushions in the meantime.

Secure in my thoughts, I tucked my head down against my
side, wrapped my fluffy tail over myself, and fell fast asleep.

Chapter
Ten

The next day, as Anya had told me, was Monday — which meant she had to go to school. She explained this to me when she climbed up the tree to bring me my breakfast, wearing a tartan skirt and a white blouse that wouldn't have looked very out of place back home in Edinburgh. I'd seen lots of schoolchildren walking past my window wearing something similar.

'But you can just wait here for me,' she said, as I polished off the food she'd put in my bowl. 'I'll be back this afternoon.'

Hmm … Waiting there didn't sound much like an adventure — in fact, it sounded just like being at home again, watching through windows until Mum or Dad returned. Plus, sitting in Anya's tree house wouldn't give me any great ideas for how to help her find a new friend, would it? Otherwise I'd have had one already.

No, if I wanted to help Anya, I needed to go with her. Everywhere. It was the only answer.

I paused for a moment as I realized this. How much I'd changed in the few short weeks since leaving Edinburgh. Before, I would *always* have chosen to stay home and wait, to watch for Anya coming back and to listen to her tell me about her day. That wasn't enough for me any more, though.

I wasn't that Lara any more.

I wondered idly what Gobi would make of the new me.

When Anya moved to climb back down the tree, I went with her. She had the ladder thing, made of rope and wood, that she used to get in and out of the tree house. The rungs were too far

123

apart for me to use, I realized, even if I stretched out. Maybe with a lot of practice at climbing … But I didn't have that yet, and I *really* didn't want to fall headfirst out of a tree. Just looking at the ladder was giving me flashbacks to my early attempts to get out of Kitty's window. And that wasn't nearly as high up as this tree.

So instead of trying to climb down, I waited in the doorway and meowed very loudly until Anya got the hint.

She stopped, halfway down the ladder, and looked up at me with those friendly hazel eyes. Then she smiled.

'You want to come with me?'

I meowed my agreement. I might not be able to actually talk to humans, but I figured my meaning was pretty clear. Still, Anya looked uncertain, so I took a step forward, feeling for the first rung of the ladder with my paw. I wasn't going to *actually* try and climb down, but she didn't know that. Panicked, she reached up and grabbed me with both hands, steadying herself on the ladder with her knees and body. 'Okay, okay, you can come down, but I won't be here to help you back up if you get cold or bored. And you *definitely* can't come to school with me.'

Which just showed how little she knew me. I might have spent most of my life in one house, behind windows, but since I'd got out, I'd been making up for it. And if I could make it all the way to Australia, a little *school* wasn't going to keep me out now, was it?

As it turned out, the school was very capable of keeping me out.

I followed Anya as she walked down her street, across some other streets and along a bit further to reach the school gates. I paid close attention to the route she took, checking trees and houses on the way, so I could find my way back if I needed to.

This neighbourhood was still very unfamiliar to me, and after my encounter with the alley cats, I wanted to make sure I could always find my way home to Anya again, however far I wandered.

Hopefully, though, I'd only be wandering *with* Anya anyway.

The school was a large, low building, with lots and lots of kids outside it, standing in groups or running around on the large concrete area, chasing a ball. *I* could do that – I'd fit right in at this school. Admittedly, the school gates were rather large and imposing, but I was confident I'd be able to walk right through them with Anya. But there was one thing I hadn't counted on. Well, two, really.

One was the caretaker. The other was his dog.

The moment I placed one paw through the gate to Anya's school, they were both there, barking at me in their own way.

'No animals allowed, you know that,' the caretaker said, his voice sharp and hard.

Anya shrugged. 'She's not mine, I can't stop her following me.' She shot me an apologetic look, but I understood. And anyway, I didn't want to get her into any more trouble.

'Well, Brutus can,' the caretaker replied.

Of course, the dog was called Brutus.

A few harsh barks, and I'd backed off, standing on the wrong side of the fence.

Anya sighed, and crouched down next to me.

'I'm sorry, Puss. I told you that you wouldn't be allowed into school with me.'

'Is she really talking to that *cat*?' A vicious voice floated over from just outside the gates. 'How hard up for friends *is* she?'

Anya and I both looked over. By the gates stood a gang of five girls, all in the same uniform as Anya – although their tartan skirts looked a lot shorter. Anya frowned at them, but her eyes didn't look annoyed, they looked nervous and a little upset.

'Personally, I feel sorry for the cat,' another of the girls said, making them all laugh.

Anya's gaze jerked away from the gang of girls and back to me.

'I'll see you later, Puss,' she said, softly, before getting to her feet. There were still tears in her eyes, though.

I couldn't let her go into school upset, and especially not with those awful girls watching. Quickly, I weaved my way through her legs, my fluffy fur brushing up comfortingly against her. I moved in a figure of eight, ensuring she couldn't move without the risk of tripping over me.

Anya laughed, a small, uncertain laugh. 'Puss! I have to go to school now.'

Not if I had anything to do with it. I didn't like the idea of her spending the day away from me anyway – and I liked it even less now I knew what it was like for her.

Those girls were mean for no other reason than they could be. Anya hadn't done anything to them, said anything to them or even *looked* at them before they started picking on her. But because she was alone, they thought she was easy prey – like I'd been for the alley cats.

Well, she wasn't alone, and I was going to show them that.

'Puss, I really need to go,' Anya said, keeping her voice low. Glancing up, I could see that the gang of girls were still watching her, and whispering in between giggles. They were laughing at her. Because of me.

I wasn't helping at all.

I stopped moving and let Anya past. I didn't want to make things even worse for her. But how was I supposed to support and look after her if I wasn't allowed to stay with her?

I watched, helplessly, as Anya walked away into a playground full of mean girls and bullies, with only a quick glance back over her shoulder at me. In no time she'd disappeared into the crowd, the girls from the gate following behind, still giggling and whispering. Anya was still alone and lonely, and there was nothing I could do to help. What use was I out here?

More to the point, what was I going to do all day without her, and with no one to feed me lunch? She was right – I still couldn't climb up to the tree house alone. And I couldn't just help myself to the cat food, even if I did.

(Seriously, when are they going to invent cat food pouches that can be opened by paws? They'd be perfect for emergencies like this.)

Slinking a little way away – at least out of barking range of Brutus the caretaker's dog – I sank back down onto my haunches in a patch of grass near the hedgerow, and thought, *Now what?*

What was I supposed to do now? What would Gobi do, or Cleo, or Dad?

What *could* I do?

I was so busy pondering how I could help Anya, and whether I really could squeeze through the bars of the fence (the whiskers said no, but I'd never really tested them before. *Maybe* it could work … or maybe I'd get stuck and the caretaker and Brutus would be responsible for getting me out, and would just stand there and laugh instead, probably along with the mean girls from the gate … Maybe I wouldn't risk it) that I almost didn't notice when Brutus moved on. At least, until I heard the caretaker bark, 'No animals allowed!' again from further along the path, the other side of the gate.

This time, the culprits were a small boy and his even smaller dog. The boy looked nervous, and the dog absolutely terrified

– but that was probably to do with Brutus. With his huge jaws and mean black eyes, he was definitely a dog to inspire terror. Fortunately, he also seemed to be as thick as two short planks, if the half-sentences he'd barked at me were anything to go by.

Despite how afraid she must be, the little dog stood firmly between her owner and Brutus, clearly indicating to the bigger dog that he'd have to go through her to get at the boy. That took some courage. I couldn't help but be secretly a little impressed.

'I'm not … I'm not bringing her in,' the boy stuttered, looking up at the caretaker with wide eyes. He was a little shorter than Anya, but about the same age, as far as I could tell. It was hard to be sure with humans. 'My mum's just parking the car. She'll come and get her. I just … Petra wanted to come with me.'

Petra. That was a good dog name, much better than Brutus. Or *Gobi*, come to that.

I slunk over, towards Petra. She was a tiny thing, not much bigger than me, and white and fluffy. About as far from Brutus's style of dog as was possible to be. I wasn't generally a fan of dogs (really, besides humans, who is?) but watching Petra standing protectively between Brutus and the boy had given me an idea.

What we had here, I decided, was a dog who loved his human. One who knew that animals *mattered* to humans. They made a difference, could help them. Something those girls at the gate certainly hadn't grasped. And suddenly I realized that was exactly what I needed to be able to help Anya.

Whenever Dad told the story of how he found Gobi, out in the desert, while running one of his races (an ultramarathon apparently, whatever one of those is. Sounds exhausting!), he always talked about how, when the race got tough, having Gobi there beside him helped him to get through it. All Gobi had to do was be there, running with him. And let's face it, if *Gobi* could do it, I definitely could. I'd just never needed to before – or wanted to.

Now I did: for Anya.

I wanted to help – I just needed a little guidance and assistance with the how.

Somewhere, a bell rang. Looking reluctant, the boy tied Petra's lead to the railing beside the gate, then knelt down beside her to say goodbye. I slunk closer to eavesdrop, making sure to keep myself hidden in the hedge so that Brutus didn't spot me.

'Mum will be here any minute,' he whispered, as he rubbed between Petra's ears. 'You just wait here for her. I have to go in … in there, now.' He looked nervously towards the school, and I saw Petra's ears flatten: she didn't like the idea of him going in there any more than he did. 'I'll be fine,' he said, unconvincingly. 'I'll see you later.'

Petra put a paw up on his leg, trying to keep him with her just as I had attempted to do with Anya. I could see tears in the boy's eyes too, and he looked thoroughly miserable at the idea of another day at school. From what I'd seen, I couldn't blame him. But if my idea worked, maybe Petra and I could make school less awful for both of them.

With a final pat, and a small yelp from Petra, the boy raced through the gates towards the school as the bell rang one more time, somehow with added urgency.

The caretaker slammed the gates closed behind him, looking vaguely disappointed that he didn't get to lock the boy out. Brutus gave a final bark for good measure, then they both headed into the school, too.

Petra sank down onto the floor, her head resting on her paws, her tail totally still as she waited for the boy's mother to come and collect her. Giving up my hiding place, I sidled closer to the little dog. She was so busy watching the disappearing boy, she didn't even notice me until I spoke.

'He doesn't seem keen to go to school today,' I observed, casually, and Petra jumped at the sound. She spun round to look at me, then relaxed, obviously deciding I was no threat. (Dogs always think cats aren't a threat, normally because they're smaller than they are. What they fail to note, of course, is our obviously superior minds. What we lack in strength, we make up for in brains and cunning. And claws and loud screeching, if it comes to that. Also, to be honest, Petra wasn't all that much bigger than me.)

'What's it to you?' she asked, suspiciously.

I gave a casual shrug of the shoulders as I paced around her. 'Nothing, really. Only my girl wasn't keen to go in this morning either. Thought it might be catching.'

'Oh, it's just that it's only Harry's second week here,' Petra explained. 'He really hasn't settled yet.'

'New school, huh?' I thought about Anya's best friend who'd moved away to a new school, too. 'Hear there's a lot of that going around.'

Petra gave me a funny look, but now she'd starting talking, it seemed she wanted to tell me all about their situation. 'We just moved to town because of his dad's job. We had to leave everything behind – our house, our garden, all Harry's friends.'

I winced. Poor Harry had it even worse than Anya, in some ways. But at least he still had Petra. 'Sounds tough.'

'It was. We're all still adjusting, I guess. You know, learning the new scents and sounds, new walk routes, that sort of thing.'

'Yeah.' I sort of understood, from my adventures so far. But on the other hand, I'd never had to move away for good before, knowing I might never go back home again. In fact, I'd never even really left Edinburgh for more than a few days until this trip.

'But you don't sound like you're from around here, either,' Petra commented, looking suspicious. I suppose my accent gave me away. Petra sounded more like the alley cats than any animals back home, so I guessed she and Harry had moved from another part of Australia, rather than across the world like me.

'Just passing through,' I said, airily, as if I went to strange new countries all the time, just for fun. Explaining exactly what I was doing in Australia would take far too long, and suddenly I had *two* children to help, not just one. Fortunately, I thought I could help both of them at once, if my new plan worked. 'So, Harry doesn't like the school?'

'It's not the school, exactly,' Petra said, with a sigh. 'He hasn't made any new friends yet, so he's lonely when I can't be with him.'

Just like Anya. Two kids with no friends. Now, that was something I might be able to help with!

I gave Petra my widest smile. 'What would you say if I told you I could help you – and Harry – settle in here?'

Petra's eyes narrowed. 'I'd ask exactly how you thought you could do that. He doesn't need another pet, you know – he already has me.'

'And I wouldn't dream of stepping on your paws,' I promised.

'Well, in that case …' Petra looked uncertain, but then gave a little nod. 'Go on, what's your big idea?'

'How do you think Harry would like to make a potential new best friend with a tree house?'

Chapter
Eleven

Harry's Mum came and grabbed Petra a few minutes later, looking flustered and upset that she hadn't been able to see her son before he went into school. I guessed that moving towns had been hard on the whole family, and they were all still adjusting.

I was also pretty sure that if Harry made even *one* friend – preferably Anya – that everyone's lives would get a little easier and happier. I'd seen before how happiness – or unhappiness – could spread through a whole family. Look at Kitty's house, where her husband's sour nature seemed to have infected everyone in that home. (Except Jennifer, of course. I wasn't sure there was anything in the world that could sour her, except maybe constant flying. She was just an eternally happy soul, always confident things would work out, even when there was no evidence at all that they would.)

Even in my own home, when Gobi was missing and Dad was so sad, it made us all sad, for a while. Next, his determination to find her became infectious, and we were all filled with the intensity of it. Then, when he finally came home after months in Beijing, his happiness – and Gobi's too, for that matter – was catching. We all smiled for days.

Until Gobi started stealing my prawns, and Mum and Dad's attention, of course.

Anyway, the point was, if I could help make Harry happy, it would follow that the rest of his family would get happier too. And if his parents were happy, that would make Harry happier still. Like one of those toys that's a ball inside a ball. As one goes around, the other does too, until you can't tell which is making it move, it's just in constant motion. For Harry's family, happiness would cause more happiness, which would cause even more happiness in turn. Easy. And by making Harry happy, I could also make Anya happier – which was my ultimate goal at the moment. And her happiness would infect Harry with more happiness and so on.

(At least, that was the theory. I'll be honest, I didn't have a lot of experience to base it on, and it was entirely possible that I'd just been infected with Jennifer's unerring optimism. But we had to try something, right? Why not this?)

We might have only had a few minutes, but that was enough for Petra and I to come up with the basics of a plan. Tomorrow morning, when the kids came to school, I'd make sure to follow Anya again and delay her from going in until Harry arrived. Then we could guide them towards meeting each other. They both had pets, so that was something in common already. And neither of them had any friends, so that was another thing they could talk about. And once they started talking, and Anya told him about her tree house, I figured it would be best friends from there on in. Easy!

Who could resist a tree house?

I purred happily at Anya as she fed me and petted me in the tree house after school.

'You must have had a good day, Puss,' she said, as she tipped the food into my bowl. 'Or at least, it must have been better than mine.'

She pulled a face and I even took a moment away from my dinner to press up against her hand in sympathy. I couldn't tell her she needn't worry about school or not having any friends any more. But she just had to wait until tomorrow, when my plan would take effect.

Anya didn't know it yet, but everything was going to work out perfectly.

Or it would have, if *I'd* been the one in control. But not being able to talk to humans definitely had its limitations.

Anya and Harry didn't understand the plan. That, or they were being deliberately difficult. (Honestly, we need a cat-to-human dictionary, it would make life *so* much easier!)

My part of the plan went off perfectly. I yowled to be taken down from the tree house until Anya agreed, then trotted alongside her all the way to the school. The route was becoming familiar already, and I enjoyed the morning stroll. In fact, I was almost skipping along with anticipation and excitement for what would happen next.

When we arrived at school, there was no sign of Harry and Petra yet, so I shamelessly begged a little extra attention from Anya until the bell rang. Anything to keep her distracted until he arrived.

'I've got to go in now, Puss,' she said, laughing, as I brushed against her hand again, not letting her move away. 'The first bell has already gone!'

Just then, I heard a bark and I knew that Petra and Harry had made it.

Perfect.

Checking to make sure that Anya was watching, I sauntered over towards Petra – who came chasing up to meet me. Always too enthusiastic, dogs, that's their problem.

'Petra!' Harry called nervously, trying to get her away from me.

I landed a playful swipe on Petra's nose, and she bounced with excitement.

'Are they playing or fighting?' Anya asked, watching us.

'I can't tell,' Harry admitted. 'But I need to get Petra tied up before I can go into school. My mum is still trying to park the car again, and Petra just wouldn't stay in there with her.'

'That's why I walk to school,' Anya said. 'Mum always says that it would take us longer to drive and park than for me to walk.'

This was good! They were talking. Next, Harry could ask her where she lived. If it was close to him, maybe they could walk together ...

But then the second bell rang, cutting short their conversation. Petra and I had been so busy listening to them talk, we'd forgotten to keep playing, and without us noticing, Harry was already tying Petra up to the fence.

'See you,' Anya said, racing through the gates the moment she saw that Harry was done.

'Bye, Petra. See you later,' he said, as he followed more slowly behind.

Petra and I watched them go.

'Well, that was a disaster,' I said.

But Petra shook her head. 'It was a start. We just need to nudge them towards the next step, now.'

'Any ideas how, exactly?' I asked, a little sarcastically.

'Your girl says she walks to school, right? Because it's not very far?' Petra asked.

I nodded. 'Only a few streets, really.'

'Hmm ... I don't think we can be all that much further away, to be honest,' Petra said.

'Why don't you just walk to school, if you're that close?'

'Harry's mum has to get to work from here. She works part-time at an animal charity, and she's allowed to take me with her, but it's a bit of a drive. I think she hoped that driving to school, then on to work would be quicker than walking to school and then back again.'

'Doesn't look like it. Maybe you could all walk, especially on the way home?' An idea was already brewing in my mind. Best of all, I could be there to make sure it all happened correctly, too. Not like at school, when I had no way to make sure Harry and Anya connected the right way.

In fact, my new plan was even better than the old plan!

Petra scrunched up her nose. 'How would I make Harry's mum decide to walk?'

Honestly, dogs! You really had to do all their thinking for them.

'I don't know! Grab your lead before it's time to leave, wave it about a bit? Something like that?'

'I suppose that could work,' Petra said, doubtfully. 'But why do you want us to walk?'

'Because that way, you'll have to be here at the gates waiting for Harry to come out, rather than waiting in the car, right?'

'I suppose. But then what? You saw what happened this morning – they said a few words, then went off in different directions. What does it matter if we're all here if they're not going to talk?'

I purred with the satisfaction of a plan well thought out. 'Trust me, my plan will do the rest.'

'And your plan is …?'

I managed to whisper most of it to her before Harry's mum arrived, looking even more flustered and annoyed than the day before. 'That's it, tomorrow you're definitely staying in the car. None of this whining and jumping and barking to distract me. Or maybe we'll just all walk – I think it might be easier at this point. I think I'm parked further away than our house today anyway!' She tugged on Petra's lead. 'Come on, now. I'm late for work!'

I watched them go, taking a moment to appreciate the brilliance of my plan. Really, it's a miracle anyone gets by without me.

I was waiting by the school gates when the bell rang once more to signal the end of the school day. In truth, I'd wandered off after Petra left to explore a bit, and keep an eye out for some food, but then spent most of the afternoon hiding from the caretaker and Brutus as I hung around, waiting for the bell. (Humans seem to have this time thing all figured out, with clocks and watches and phones and stuff. Us animals just have to rely on our stomachs, and having skipped lunch, I might have predicted an afternoon snack a little early. It's hard to rely on an empty belly when it comes to telling the time!)

I saw Petra and Harry's mum first, walking from a different direction to where she'd appeared from that morning. I hoped that meant they'd walked to the school, and it really wasn't too far from Anya's house. Now, I was just hoping that Anya and Harry would appear at the gates around the same time. Otherwise things could be tricky.

Anya appeared first, bursting into a smile when she saw me waiting for her. I let her make a fuss of me for a few moments, keeping an eye out for Harry the whole time.

Petra spotted him first and barked to alert me, as we'd arranged. I jumped up at the sound, surprising Anya, who almost lost her balance. I felt bad about that, but it couldn't be helped – I needed to be ready to action the plan the moment the circumstances were exactly right.

I had a feeling that Anya and Harry might be just a little bit cross at my plan. But that was only because we couldn't explain to them how we were helping them, really. In the absence of a shared language, we had to rely on actions.

And my superb planning skills, of course.

We waited until Harry had greeted his mum and taken Petra's lead from her. He looked relieved to be out of school again, and bent down to make a fuss of Petra until his mum started getting impatient. As soon as he stood up again, Petra gave me the nod, and I started to run.

'Puss!' Anya called after me. 'Where are you going?'

Ignoring her (I mean, it wasn't like I could actually answer her anyway), I raced off in the direction of Anya's house, glancing back over my shoulder to make sure the plan was working as I went.

Barking wildly, Petra wrenched her lead from Harry's hand and chased after me. Shouts went up from Harry and Anya, and I could see from her face that Harry's mum was grumbling, even if I couldn't hear the words. She didn't matter, anyway. Both kids were racing after Petra and me now – and that was the important thing. It was all going perfectly!

I was glad now I'd taken the time to memorize our usual route between home and school. There was no time to think about which way I needed to go, or which turning was the right one. I just had to run and run, and trust Petra to follow and lead the others after us. *Everything* depended on Petra and I reaching the tree house before the children did.

Petra made sure not to get too close until we were almost at Anya's house. Then she closed in, just as I skidded around the corner into the back garden. The kids were catching up now too, but that was okay. We were nearly there – and Harry's mum was far enough behind that, while she could still see us, it would take her a bit to catch up. There was no way she could stop us now.

Hopping up onto one of the lower rungs of the ladder, just outside Petra's reach, I perched and looked down at her. She was still playing the part, yapping loudly and bouncing up and down, trying to reach me. Actually, perhaps she'd forgotten this was a plan at all, and just got caught up in the chase. It wouldn't surprise me, from a dog.

It didn't make a difference, anyway: the plan had worked.

Out of breath and panting, Anya and Harry arrived in the garden together. Harry went straight to Petra's side, grabbing her lead and wrapping it around his hand securely. Anya rushed to the rope ladder to check I was okay. I tried to look trauma-tised by the experience, rather than just smug my plan had worked.

'I'm really, really sorry,' Harry said to Anya. His eyes were wide, and he kept chewing his lower lip, like he was afraid Anya would be cross with him. Luckily, I knew her better than that. 'Petra *never* runs or chases usually. I don't know what's up with her. Maybe she's still unsettled after the move here. Strange new town and everything …'

'You're new at school, right?' Anya asked, leaning up against the tree next to me and stroking my fur slowly. She was proba-bly trying to calm me down. An *ordinary* cat would have been terrified after that chase. Not me, though – I was just excited for Anya to make a new friend.

'That's right,' Harry said, with a nod. 'Just moved last week.'

'What do you think of Bellamy High?'

Harry pulled a face, and Anya laughed. 'Me too,' she said.

'It would be better if anyone wanted to make friends,' Harry said. 'But everyone seems to have their friends and groups already, and there's no room for the new kid.'

'I know how you feel,' Anya replied. 'My best friend moved away last term, so now it's just me. Well, me and Puss, here.' She patted my fur, as the two of them eyed each other carefully. They were so nearly there …

Then Harry's attention got pulled away. 'Hey, is that a tree house?'

Anya beamed. 'Yep. Want to come up?'

'Yeah!'

By the time Harry's mum arrived, a few minutes later, Anya and Harry were already new best friends, and making plans for a sleepover in the tree house.

Never let it be said that I am not a *genius* among cats.

 # Gobi

The 'Bring Lara Home' campaign had developed a life of its own since we returned home to Edinburgh. From us being the only people in the world who cared about our missing cat – well, us and Françoise at the airport – suddenly, people were sending in photo after photo of Ragdoll cats from all over the world. There were Ragdolls in Paris, or further afield in France, but also ones from England, America, Germany, India, Japan, Russia, even Australia! But none of them were Lara. Dion and I – and sometimes Lucja too – were on TV and radio shows every few days, talking about my missing sister and how important it

was to get her home again. Dion almost lost his voice from all the talking.

Most people we spoke to were supportive, and desperate to help, but some thought that while losing one pet was understandable, losing two was just irresponsible. I resisted the urge to bite those people, only because I knew Dion and Lucja wouldn't like it.

One day, as I sat on another TV sofa (which was loads more uncomfortable than our sofa at home, incidentally), I imagined Lara out there somewhere, maybe even sitting on another sofa, watching me on the telly. Who was she with? Who was taking care of her? Was she really watching? If she was, I hoped she could see how much we all missed her, and needed her home with us. And I really hoped she would find a way to make it happen. Because as hard as Dion and Lucja were working to bring Lara home, I'd realized something that they hadn't yet: Lara could come home any time she chose. She was clever, resourceful, and the whole world was looking for her.

If she wanted to come back, she just had to find someone to read her microchip and realize it was her, and she'd be on her way. In an airport in Paris – or wherever she flew to – that should have been easy. In fact, it would be much harder to keep hidden than to let herself be caught.

The fact that she hadn't been caught told me she wasn't ready to come home just yet.

I didn't know what my sister was looking for, out there in the big, wide world, but I really hoped that she found it soon – I missed her.

The first glimmer of hope we'd had in days arrived very late one Saturday night, when I was snoozing on the sofa in our Edinburgh flat, next to Lucja as she watched something on the telly. It was much easier to sleep through TV programmes without Lara there, talking all the way through them, I'd realized. Still, I missed her chatter.

'Lucja! Lucja, we've got an email!'

I jerked awake at the sound of Dion calling for his wife. Beside me on the sofa, Lucja patted my side to settle me back down, and I turned around a few times to get comfortable beside her again.

But I wasn't settling – I was listening, very carefully.

'An email? Dion, we get thousands of those a day! What makes this one any different?' she asked.

He bounced on his toes in front of the sofa, holding out the tablet for her to read for herself. 'The woman writing says she travelled from Paris – the same airport as us, on the very same day – with a cat that looked just like Lara. The flight was going to Australia!'

Dion sounded more excited than I'd heard him in weeks. Lucja, however, wasn't joining in with his high spirits.

'Australia? Dion, Jennifer was going to Australia.' *When he looked at her blankly, she sighed and explained.* 'Jennifer? The woman we gave a lift to the airport? The woman with the Ragdoll cat who looked just like Lara …?'

Dion sank down onto the sofa beside us. 'Oh, so you think the cat this woman saw was …?'

'Cleo,' *Lucja confirmed with a nod.* 'Jennifer's cat. Yes.'

Lucja might not be excited, but I was. Because if Cleo was the cat that Françoise had found at the airport, then that meant Lara had to be the cat on the plane! I'd seen her in Jennifer's carrier, but I'd hoped she'd escaped. If she hadn't, she must be in Australia!

I wanted to shout at Dion and Lucja, to bark at them to think it through and reach the same conclusion I had. I'd never regretted not being able to speak human more in my life. Fortunately, I was found and fostered by very intelligent humans. It took them a moment, but they got there.

'Wait,' *Dion said.* 'But if Cleo was on the plane, where did the Ragdoll cat they found at the airport come from? They said the microchip data was out of date, so they couldn't contact the owner. But it had to be Cleo, right? With her and Lara, that's already two Ragdoll cats wandering around one airport. Statistically, how many more could there be?'

'It does seem unlikely,' Lucja admitted. 'But that would mean ...'

'That the cat on the plane really was Lara!' Dion finished for her. 'But how?'

Lucja frowned, the way she always did when she was thinking something through. 'What if Jennifer took Lara by mistake, instead of Cleo? They had that little tussle, remember? Just after we went through security.'

'But that would mean that the cat that ran away from us wasn't Lara at all – it was Cleo.'

They stared at each other, while I spun around between them, the excitement almost too much. They'd got it. They finally understood what was going on.

Maybe now we could find Lara, ask her to come home!

'I can't see any other way it could have happened,' Dion said, eventually. 'Can you?'

Lucja shook her head. 'Which means we need to find Jennifer.'

Dion pulled up the web browser on his tablet. 'Already on it.'

I settled down beside him, happier than I'd felt in weeks.

Lara would be home in no time, I was sure of it.

Chapter
Twelve

Harry had been round to play after school every day for a week. Sometimes he brought Petra, sometimes he came alone, but since I was the only animal allowed in the tree house, I didn't mind so much. The kids seemed to be getting along well, much better than I'd even hoped for when I'd come up with the whole plan. Apparently, they had more in common than loneliness, pets and a love of tree houses, which helped. I honestly believed that they might be friends for life.

Petra and I had done a good thing here, even if our humans never realized that we were behind it. They probably thought they'd made friends all on their own!

My good deed left a warm, happy feeling in my belly that had nothing to do with the extra afternoon snack Harry had fed me when Anya wasn't looking: I'd helped another person, and that felt good. It felt like I'd found what I was meant to do, the adventure I was meant to have. That happy feeling stayed with me the whole week – until the day I realized it was time for me to move on again.

Anya and Harry were playing some complicated game with cards and dice in the tree house, and it occurred to me that I'd never seen her look so relaxed and contented. Not even when she brought me home. She'd been pleased to have me with her, of course – for the company, or the reminder of Millie, the cat who had died. But there'd always been a sadness about it too. Because I wasn't her pet, not really. Her parents still didn't know about me, and the supply of leftover cat food I was relying on had to run out sometime. What would happen then? Would

Anya talk to her parents, try to find more? Or would she forget about me, now that she had Harry to keep her company instead?

No, Anya wouldn't do that. She'd try to find a way to help me, I was sure. But she was still only a child. If her parents said no, that would be the end of it.

Harry was hers – her friend, legitimately. She had someone now.

Which meant she didn't need me any more.

And besides, hanging out with two kids in a tree house, and a yappy little dog the rest of the time, wasn't exactly the grand adventure I'd been searching for, was it? I'd done what I'd hoped to do here – found Anya a friend.

Now it was time to get back to looking for my *own* adventure. One that would outdo anything Gobi had achieved, and prove once and for all that I was the top pet in our household. Once I got home again. Somehow.

I didn't dwell on the logistics. It was time for more new places, new people and new experiences. And maybe I'd even find someone else who needed my help, too. That would be good.

It seemed this helping people thing was sort of addictive.

I'd used my time at Anya's wisely, learning some very important tricks. Starting with how to climb down a tree.

My decision made, there didn't seem much point in wasting any more time. I was well fed, well rested, and Anya was happy and distracted. It was as good a time as any to leave and I might even be able to find somewhere to stop for the night and get some food and rest before the sun went down, if I hit the road now.

I brushed up against Anya for one last pet, then headed out on my own, down the ladder and out into the world. Anya might not have known it was goodbye, but I did, and that was enough. She had Harry and Petra now, she'd soon forget about me.

Petra was sitting at the bottom of the ladder, waiting for Harry to get bored and resume their walk, I presumed.

'Where are you off to?' she asked, as I descended (almost) gracefully from the tree house.

'Time to move on,' I replied. 'I told you I was only passing through.'

'Yeah, but ...' Petra glanced up at the tree house as a burst of laughter floated down from the children. 'Won't Anya miss you? And, I mean, won't you miss Anya, too?'

'Perhaps. But this isn't my home, Petra. And it's not what I came to Australia for.'

'What did you come here for then?' Petra looked puzzled. 'I mean, if it wasn't for a home and a human to love you, what else is there?'

'Adventure.' Even the word sounded exciting to me now. When I'd first set off from Edinburgh, I'd been nervous, unsure. Even when I'd left Jennifer, I hadn't known how I would feed myself or where I'd sleep, and that had felt terrifying. But now, all those things seemed possible. I'd practised foraging for food during the day while Anya was at school, catching the occasional rodent or bird (okay, putting one or two out of their misery after some accident or other, most of the time) and checking out the local bins (watching out for alley cats as I did so). But more importantly, I knew now that there was always something – and someone – new around each corner.

Perhaps I didn't know where I was going next, but maybe that was all part of the fun. Wherever it was, I was sure I'd find someone to open me a tin of fish, or a warm spot to sun myself in during the day. I'd be fine.

I could make it on my own.

And knowing that, I realized, was the real freedom I thought I'd found when I left Kitty's house.

'Adventure,' Petra repeated, and shuddered. 'No, thank you! I like a warm bed and a regular meal schedule.'

'I thought I did too,' I admitted. 'But that was before.'

'Before what?'

I considered my answer for a moment. 'Before Gobi, I suppose.'

And before Petra could ask who or what Gobi was, I waved my tail in farewell, and disappeared through the trees towards my next adventure.

I hit the road again with my new-found confidence still running high. For the next day or so I took my time meandering through neighbourhoods, exploring new surroundings. At night, I slept under hedges, or inside unlocked garden sheds. During the day, I discovered the wonder of cat flaps, and my ability to nip through them and share another cat's food. (I figured they probably wouldn't mind, they had humans to feed them more, right?) I also learned to be very careful in making sure those other cats – or their humans – weren't at home when I did it. (Some weren't quite as unbothered by it as I'd hoped.)

This continued until the morning I stumbled upon a train station. It looked a lot like the one Jennifer had taken me through a few times when we'd travelled into the city together – in fact, I was almost certain that it was the same one. Somehow, in all my wanderings, I'd found my way back to the same neighbourhood that Jennifer was staying in.

I stood on the platform, weighing up my options. From here, I could find my way back to Kitty's house, and Jennifer, if she was still visiting. I could see if Jennifer had completed her quest and found somewhere to scatter Jeremy's ashes. I could even travel home with her, back to Britain, when she was ready to go.

Or, I could hop on the next train into the city, and see where adventure took me next.

Decisions, decisions ...

With a screech and a hiss, a train pulled into the station. After a moment, the doors opened, and a crowd of people got off. I considered for one more second, then the doors beeped to say they were closing.

I was here for an adventure, I reminded myself. And that meant there really wasn't a choice to be made at all.

I jumped between the closing doors before they met in the middle and strolled along the carriage to find a comfortable seat. As ever, people noticed me go – I'm a noticeable kind of cat.

'Think it's got a ticket?' one mum asked her two children, who giggled. I raised my nose and tail and ignored them. I don't know why humans think they're the only ones with a right to space in this world. (And I had no idea how to get one of those ticket things Jennifer had acquired from the machines on the platform, anyway.)

The train had really interesting windows to look out of. Not quite as good as the plane, but still interesting. I stood with my paws against the glass, my hind legs on the seat cushion, and watched as the city streamed past us. Homes and shops and cars and people and trees and dogs on leads and birds pecking for food and plenty more. It made me realize how much more of the world there still was for me to see. How could I have even thought of stopping adventuring now?

Eventually, the train reached the end of the line – the same station I'd travelled into with Jennifer, just a week or two before. As the passengers streamed out of the train doors, I weaved my way through their legs to find my own path out into the city.

The midday sun was high in the sky, warm and welcoming without being so hot the only thing to do was bask. The pavement was warm under my paws as I padded along the city streets. It felt different, seeing the city without being tethered to a harness. I wasn't limited to only going where Jennifer wanted to go – or even to places that a human was allowed. I could look down on the city from atop walls, or sneak through gaps into places humans didn't even know existed.

The freedom went to my head a little, and I slipped through some railings into the grounds of a large building – maybe an office, I thought. Hopping from windowsill to wall, and from fire escape to ledge, I made my way all the way up to the roof of the building, and stared out over the city of Sydney.

The sun shone off the harbour and the shells that made up the bright white roof of the opera house. Out on the water, tiny boats bobbed about further out, sailing towards the islands beyond. Down below, people scurried around on the street, as small as mice to me from my vantage place. I took a moment to let it all sink in.

How far I'd come from my existence behind those windows in Edinburgh.

Now I was here, nothing could stop me.

Well, nothing except the fire escape on the roof banging open and a large man coming out and lighting up a cigarette. I leapt back down from ledge to ledge, back to street level, ready to continue my journey.

With no real destination in mind, I found myself revisiting some of the places I'd gone with Jennifer, seeing them again for myself, without having to follow her around. Harness-free, the Botanic Gardens were a whole new world of hidey-holes and mazes and adventures, in and around the shrubs and plants. I spent a happy afternoon sunning myself on a bright patch of grass near a cafe, helping myself to any tasty-looking leftovers, and getting plenty of attention from the patrons. Fed and nicely petted, I carried on once it got dark, and found a comfy and cosy mossy patch under a still-green leaved bush to sleep for the night.

The next day, I continued exploring. I decided to give the Harbour Bridge a miss this time around, but I did find myself wandering past the Queen Victoria Building again.

As I realized where I was, I backtracked a little – and spotted what I was looking for.

There, sitting on his little stone plinth, underneath an iron-work canopy, was Islay. Queen Victoria's Cairn terrier, and apparently, her favourite pet. Unconstrained by a harness this time, I hopped up onto the wall surrounding the well below him (balancing very, very carefully).

'Hello, my name is Islay. I was once the companion and friend of the great Queen Victoria.' The words started up automatically, exactly the same as before. I assumed it was sort of like the radio at home, just playing on repeat.

Islay wasn't a *real* dog – not this version of him, anyway. But somehow, something about him reminded me of Gobi. Maybe it was the way he sat waiting for people to pay him attention and throw money in his well.

'Because of the many good deeds I have done for deaf and blind children, I have been given the power of speech,' Islay went on.

Or, and I had to admit this was more likely, perhaps it was how he was raising money to help others, according to the information Jennifer had read from her guidebook.

Gobi had helped Dad in the desert, and Mum always said she'd inspired thousands of other people too, with her adventures. I had a feeling Gobi would like Islay.

'If you cast a coin into the wishing well now, I will say thank you.'

'I don't have a coin,' I told the little dog. I didn't know if statues could really hear people or animals talking to them, but it seemed only polite to answer him, just in case. 'But I'll remember you, as I go on my adventures.' Maybe I could help more people, too, the way I'd helped Anya. I'd like that – and I thought Islay would too.

'Thank you. Woof, woof!' said Islay.

I nodded to him, and hopped down, ready to continue my wanderings.

As I left, I heard a small boy say, 'Did you see that, Mum? The cat was talking to the dog statue!' He seemed delighted, so at least I'd made someone happy today.

It was easy when you knew how.

All things considered, I was feeling quite smug about how well my adventures were going – until another window gave me pause.

I was strolling down a busy street full of shops selling everything from clothes to Sydney tea towels to electronics. I'd wandered away from the city centre a bit into areas Jennifer had never explored, so I was enjoying all the new sights and sounds – not to mention all the people. Suddenly, a burst of light and movement caught my attention, and I stopped to look in the window of a shop full of TVs, computers and tablets, all showing the same image as they sat facing out to the street.

A whirl of colour across the many screens faded away to reveal three people sitting on sofas. Three humans – and one small, scruffy dog. My heart jumped at the sight, the last thing I expected to see all the way here in Australia!

Resting my paws against the windowsill, I stared up at my family – Mum and Dad and Gobi – talking to the third person, a stranger.

A strange tightness took over my chest at the unexpected sighting. Longing flooded through me – for people who knew my real name, who fed me prawns, who curled up with me at night. For all that I was loving my journey, and my freedom, in that moment all I wanted in the world was for the adventure to be over and for me to be home in Edinburgh again. With my real family.

I shook the feeling away, and focussed on reality. I was having a *fantastic* adventure and they – well, they were doing what they always did: carrying on without me. They were on TV, after all! Not sitting around, pining for me.

I couldn't hear what they were saying, but I could guess well enough. Gobi would be showing off, as usual, and they'd all be talking about her brilliant adventures, all the places she'd been and the things she'd done. If only they knew about *my* adventures. I'd have to make sure they found out all about them, somehow, when I did finally go home.

If they'd even noticed I'd gone away at all.

Disheartened at the thought that they weren't missing me in the slightest, I turned away and headed off to find something to eat and somewhere to sleep.

I didn't need a family anyway. Not when I had adventures to enjoy and a whole city to explore.

I did need supper, though.

Chapter
Thirteen

The city, I'd discovered quickly, wasn't quite so welcoming as the suburbs. Things moved faster – cars and bikes and buses that didn't seem to ever stop to let a cat cross the roads. Humans moved faster too, pushing past each other in their rush to get to wherever they were going. Plus, more buildings were offices and shops, rather than homes, so finding a friendly face to take me in was more difficult. I spent another day or two ransacking bins, hiding from alley cats of the sort I'd met on my first day out on my own, and cosying up to likely-looking humans. Every time, though, they'd stroke me and make a fuss – then walk off and leave me alone again.

This was not what I'd been hoping for.

On the third morning after I saw my family on TV, I stumbled across another window, this time the window of a bookshop. I was starting to think that the city was mocking me because, there on a stand behind the glass, was a dog-eared copy of Gobi's book, *Finding Gobi*. Her picture – black nose, trusting eyes and weird ears – stared back at me. Famous even here, on the other side of the world. Her adventures in print, for all humans to read.

While *my* adventures had stalled, and I was starting to think that nobody cared about me having them at all.

I'd wanted to prove something to Mum and Dad. But how could I do that if they hadn't even noticed I'd gone? If they truly missed me, the way they missed Gobi when she was lost, they wouldn't have been making television appearances and going on tour as if nothing had happened, would they?

I hadn't realized it when I'd decided to run away with Jennifer, but perhaps I'd been hoping to provoke a reaction. To remind Mum and Dad how much they loved me, how much they'd miss me if I wasn't there. Except obviously they didn't. And even the windows of the city seemed intent on reminding me of that fact, now.

I was about to keep on walking when the door to the bookshop opened, and a man in a brown cardigan stepped out. The cardigan matched his brown hair, and his kind brown eyes. Overall, though, he looked as tatty as the books in the window of his shop – like he'd been well read, then put down and forgotten about when the reader was done.

I knew how he felt.

'Hello, there. Looking for something to read?' He gave a quiet snort of laughter at his own joke. 'You might be the only person in this neighbourhood who is.'

I tilted my head to study him. Was he talking to me? If so, he was the first person in this city to take that kind of time and interest in a wandering cat. And if he *was* talking to me, that probably meant he didn't have anyone else to talk to – especially if no one ever came to his shop to buy books.

Maybe he needed company, and someone to talk to – just like Anya had. So many lonely people seemed to find comfort and company in animals. And families too, come to that. But if this man was lonely, maybe I could help him with that.

For a price, of course. A fishy price.

As much as I liked helping people, even I couldn't be all that helpful on an empty belly.

As if he'd read my mind, the man said, 'I bet you'd like some sardines, wouldn't you? And it just so happens I have a tin in my cupboard. Fancy some?'

I hadn't tried sardines before, but they sounded like food, so I trotted through the door he held open for me and waited to see what they tasted like.

He snorted another laugh as he watched me go, my tail high and my nose sniffing for fish. I don't know what he thought was so funny. Maybe just the idea of holding a conversation with a cat.

Inside, the shop was even shabbier than outside. The wooden floor was scratched under my paws, and dust motes danced and shone in the sunlight forcing its way through the grubby windows. The main room was lined with shelves, and every shelf crammed with books. If they were in any sort of order I couldn't tell what it was, and even if they were, there were so many shoved sideways on top of each other, or hidden behind other books, it couldn't have been easy to find anything. And that was before you even started on the piles of books on the floor.

In one corner, some cheerfully coloured bunting had been strung across the ceiling, and a pile of beanbags and cushions in primary colours was stacked on the floor, against more book-shelves. Some of these shelves held larger, thinner books with drawn pictures on the covers and big words. There were also posters featuring a girl in a suit of armour rescuing a dragon, and a boy chasing butterflies with a net. I guessed this was the children's corner – even if more of the grown-up books had been stacked up around it.

None of the books anywhere in the shop looked new – spines were cracked and covers and pages bent over in many cases. I guessed this was a shop for selling used books, so new readers could enjoy them.

I'd never really understood the appeal of books, not being able to read. But between them and the cushions in the kids' area and the rugs scattered around on the wooden floor, they did make the shop feel cosy and comforting. A bit like the man himself.

Yes, if I needed a place in the city to rest for a few days – and maybe even find a way to help someone new – I could do a lot worse than this bookshop, I decided. Especially if the sardines turned out to be worth eating.

I carefully picked my way between two towers of books, and followed him into the tiny kitchen behind the main shop. There was a sign on the door, but I couldn't read it. Maybe if I hung around in a bookshop long enough I'd learn how. *That* would be something Gobi definitely couldn't do.

'I'm Ben, by the way,' he said, in a friendly tone, as he rooted around in the cupboards. 'This, in case you hadn't guessed already, is my shop. Aha! I knew they were in here somewhere.'

He pulled out a small tin, tugged the ring pull to open it, and emptied the contents into a plastic bowl before mashing them slightly with a bent fork.

'Your dinner, Your Highness.' He placed the bowl on the floor, and I tucked in.

(Sardines, it turns out, fall somewhere above tinned cat food, but just below prawns in my list of things that Lara likes best. A definite win for the humble sardine.)

Ben perched himself on the narrow kitchen counter and watched me eat. 'I wonder what your name is. You definitely look regal – Princess, maybe?' I shot him a look, thinking of the alley cats, then returned my attention to where it belonged – my fish. 'No, you're right, too sparkly. How about … Elizabeth?'

I pulled a face, but didn't look up this time. It wasn't Lara, but it would do, I supposed. And it could definitely be worse. Really, *Princess*.

'Yes, I think Elizabeth suits you,' he said, sounding very pleased with himself. 'And you know, I've always felt that what this bookshop was lacking was a cat. Along with, well, customers, a decent revenue stream, and some proper organization. Oh, and a cleaner. But it's good to start with the little things and build up to the bigger ones, right? So, shop cat. Ticked off the list, perfect!'

I was starting to think that Ben was perfectly happy talking to himself, but if listening to him got me fish, I was happy to oblige. Besides, he *did* need a shop cat, right? He'd just said so. I was being helpful just by being here.

Licking out the last of the sardines from the bowl, I looked up at him hopefully. He sighed, and scritched between my ears, which was nice enough but didn't fill an empty belly. All that adventuring around the city had left me ravenous.

'Guess I'm going to have to go shopping for more fish then, huh?' he said. I purred in response. 'What are your favourites, I wonder?'

I thought 'prawns' very hard, and hoped for the best.

Ben hopped down from the counter and grabbed his keys and wallet from a large wooden bowl on the windowsill. 'Anything else you need, Your Majesty?' I thought 'prawns' again. 'Right, well, keep the shop warm for me. I'll be right back.'

I followed him back out into the shop, and watched as he flipped the sign on the door to 'Closed' and stepped outside. I decided to use my time alone to investigate the shop properly. I padded through the rows of shelves, the hidden corners piled with more books, and even discovered a staircase leading up to a door. There was a chain across the bottom of the stairs, which I ignored by virtue of being small enough to pass straight under it, even with my tail held high. When I reached the top, I nudged the door with my nose, but it was too tightly closed to open under the pressure. Resigned to waiting until Ben opened it for me, I returned to the shop and the battered old leather armchair in a sunny spot by the door I'd spotted earlier. It had only a couple of books on either arm, with the main cushion clear and warm, so I happily curled up for a snooze while I waited.

Ben returned with packets of what had to be every single flavour of cat food they had in the shop, judging by the colours on the front, plus a few tins I assumed contained more sardines, but no prawns.

Oh well … Until I perfected cat-to-human communication, I supposed this was as good as it was going to get. And it was a whole lot better than foraging around in rubbish bins.

'I hope you're going to hang around now I've got all this stuff in for you,' he said, pulling a small mouse from his pocket. The mouse was red and yellow and it jingled when he shook it. I jumped up for it instantly, before his words sunk in.

Ben wanted me to stay with him! He'd only known me for an afternoon, and he already wanted me to make a home at the bookshop. He'd said it like it was a joke, but I could hear the hopeful note underneath his words. He really wanted me to stay – and not just because he'd bought cat food, or because all bookshops should have their own cat.

I'd been right with my first impression: Ben was lonely, he needed company even more than he needed customers. But maybe I could find him both …

'Hungry again?' he asked. I jumped down from my chair and headed for the kitchen in response.

But while I ate my chicken and vegetable mush (that's what Ben said it was, anyway), I was already busy formulating a plan.

After all, I'd helped Anya and that had felt good. I'd promised Islay I'd try and find more people to help. Why not start by helping Ben?

When it got dark outside, Ben locked up the shop door with a key and two bolts, pulling a shade down over the glass. (I wondered why he bothered. If no one had wanted to come inside while it was daytime, why on earth would they want to at night? Besides, the glass was so dirty, it was almost impossible to see through it anyway.)

'I have a flat upstairs,' he said, looking down at me, where I'd made myself comfortable again on the armchair, ignoring the cat bed he'd laid out on the floor beside it. 'I'm going to head up there now and get ready for bed. You're welcome to join me, but you seem pretty happy here. Shall I put some water in the kitchen in case you get thirsty in the night?'

I meowed my agreement, and he wandered off, shaking his head and muttering as he headed up the stairs to the closed door I'd discovered earlier. 'Honestly! I'd thought that I couldn't get any more pathetic, but here we are. Talking to the stray cat like it can actually answer me.'

I listened to him pottering about the shop; the creak of the stairs, the footfalls from the floorboards above me, the click of a light switch as the whole place went dark. I liked Ben. He needed help, but I liked him. And there were definitely worse places to spend a few days of my adventure than curled up in the warm leather armchair.

All the same, once the shop was totally dark and silent, it did feel just a little bit lonely. I liked my armchair well enough, but maybe I should have gone up to the flat with Ben after all.

Maybe I still could … except when I looked, the door at the top of the stairs was shut again.

I was alone.

My family were thousands of miles away across oceans, living their lives without me and not even noticing I was missing. Jennifer was with her family, Anya was with Harry, and even Ben had gone upstairs and locked the door on me.

No, that wasn't fair – I'd chosen to stay down here. And I'd chosen to leave Anya, and Jennifer, and even Mum and Dad. I wasn't alone, I was adventuring solo.

I had to remember that.

As I blinked in the darkness, trying not to let it overwhelm me, I remembered what had first drawn my attention to the bookshop in the first place: the picture of my dog sister in the window.

It was just a picture. Only a book, like all the others in the shop. It didn't have any extra comforting qualities, just because it had a photo of Gobi on the front.

All the same …

Dropping down from the armchair, I padded over to the window, and slipped between two boxes displaying books until I found what I wanted. Even in the faint light from the street-light outside, barely piercing the grubby window glass, I could make out Gobi's eyes and ears on the book cover.

Carefully, using a combination of teeth and paws, I batted the copy of Gobi's book down from its stand, and dragged it over to the pile of brightly coloured cushions and beanbags in the children's section, before curling up on the softness there.

Not that I missed her or anything. Maybe I just didn't think Gobi's face was going to draw in the customers Ben needed, that was all. And if I slept with Gobi's book under my paws, my tail wrapped around me and the spine of the book, that was no one's business but my own.

 Gobi

'We were right,' Dion said, as he put the phone down. My ears pricked up, and I trotted over to his side to hear more.

'The cat at the airport?' Lucja asked, sitting up a bit straighter.

Dion nodded. 'She's the clue we've been waiting for. When they told me originally that the microchip data was out of date, I didn't ask any more questions, because I knew that Lara's was up to date.'

'And we were pretty sure that the cat in the photo wasn't Lara anyway,' Lucja reminded him.

'I know, I know. But I should have asked more questions.' Dion shook his head, and ran a hand over the back of his neck. 'It turns out that just the phone number was out of service, and so they assumed the address was an old one, too. But the name, that they could check. It took some persuading for them to do it – data protection and all that – but I talked them into it.'

'And was it Jennifer?' Lucja asked.

We both waited, tense, for his answer.

'It was Jennifer, she was the cat's owner.'

Lucja blew out a long breath. I kept on holding mine a moment longer, I needed to know what happened next.

'So, if it was definitely Cleo in the airport, then it had to be Lara on the plane with Jennifer,' Lucja concluded.

'Exactly. Except they can't give me her contact details – and even if they could, they're out of date, remember? So, they've got no way of contacting her to tell her she's got the wrong cat, either.'

'So, what do we do now?'

I was wondering the same thing. What good did it do us to know that Lara had travelled to Australia with Jennifer if we couldn't contact her? We were still in Edinburgh, thousands of miles away.

Dion pulled out a notebook and a pen. 'Now we try to remember everything that Jennifer told us about herself, and where she was going. We're going to track her down, Lucja. Her and Lara.'

I barked my agreement, and they both laughed.

'Looks like Gobi is ready to help!' Lucja joked.

She was right, though – I was.

'Okay, so we know that Jennifer was widowed, travelling alone—' Dion started.

'Except for Cleo,' Lucja interrupted, and Dion made a note on his list.

'Except for Cleo,' he repeated. 'And she was looking for somewhere to scatter her husband's ashes.'

'Oh! And she was going to stay with her daughter, I think,' Lucja added. 'Or her son. I'm not really sure.'

Dion sighed. 'It's not a lot to go on, is it?'

'Not really.'

I sank down into the cushion between them on the sofa, hope fading as fast as it had risen. This was impossible.

'Maybe we can contact the airline again? Or, no, we need to talk to the woman who emailed us first,' Lucja suggested. 'If we talk to her, we can get the flight details. Then we can see if the airline can give us her information – a surname, at least. That might help.'

'Maybe,' Dion said. But he didn't sound convinced.

I couldn't blame him. We all knew it was a long shot. Finding one woman called Jennifer in a country as big as Australia was about as impossible as finding one Ragdoll cat somewhere in the world.

'I just keep thinking, if Lara's in Australia, we should be too,' Dion said softly.

I knew exactly how he felt. Even if we didn't know exactly where she was, just being in the same country would be something.

Lucja took Dion's hand, her eyes concerned. 'Are you sure? You haven't been back there in a long time.'

'I know. But if that's where Lara is — where part of our family is …'

'Then it's where we need to be, too.' Lucja nodded. 'I'll start looking at flights, right away. And the rules about flying with animals …'

Excitement warred with nerves in my belly. I wanted to go to wherever Lara was, just as much as Dion. But I couldn't help but think there was probably a reason we hadn't been to Australia before …

I was right.

It turned out that getting me into Australia was a lot more complicated than anyone had anticipated. Luckily, I'd had a lot of the relevant jabs and checks before our China trip, so that speeded things up a little bit. All the same, it took weeks to get everything sorted.

The worst part was, I'd have to travel in the hold of the plane.

'Not the whole way,' Lucja explained to Dion and me. 'We can do as we usually do and take a ferry over to France before flying out with Gobi in the cabin with us. Then we can find somewhere to layover and—'

'Lock Gobi up in the hold for hours on end while we fly in the cabin.' Dion shook his head. 'I can't do it, Lucja. You didn't see her after she had to travel in the hold in China. She was terrified, poor thing.'

'I know, I know.' Lucja looked down at the stack of notes in her hand. 'I just can't see any other way to do it. Animals aren't allowed

into Australia travelling in the cabins of planes, unless they're an assistance dog, which Gobi isn't. And she'll have to go into quarantine in Melbourne, too, for 10 whole days.'

'Then we can't take her,' Dion said, firmly. 'We'll have to come up with something else. Find somewhere for her to stay while we go to Australia.'

No! They couldn't seriously be thinking of leaving me behind while they went to fetch Lara home? I needed to be there!

'Maybe we could leave her with friends here in Edinburgh,' Lucja suggested. 'Except if we don't have Gobi with us, we probably won't have as much success persuading the local media to help out.'

'The media do love Gobi,' Dion admitted. 'But still, I'm not sure I can force her to fly that way again.'

Force me? I was desperate to go with them. Whatever it took ...

This had gone far enough.

I barked, loudly enough to get their attention. They looked at me, mirrored surprise on their faces.

'I think Gobi has an opinion on this,' Dion said, a smile tugging at his lips.

I barked again – I most definitely did.

'Do you think she really understands what we're saying?' Lucja asked, her head tilted to one side as she looked at me.

'Of course she does, she's the cleverest dog on the planet!' Dion said. Which might be a bit of an exaggeration, but if it meant they'd listen to me on this, I'd go along with it.

'So, what's she trying to tell us, then?' Lucja sounded disbelieving.

'Maybe that she doesn't want to travel in the hold of a plane again?' Dion guessed.

I barked crossly. That wasn't it at all!

'Or not,' he added, hurriedly. 'What is it, Gobi? You want to come with us to bring Lara home?'

172

I sat down and looked at them calmly, hoping they'd interpret the move correctly.

'I think that's a "yes",' Lucja said softly.

'Even if it means travelling in the hold?' Dion asked.

I stayed still. They looked at each other.

'I guess I'd better start looking at planes to Melbourne, then,' Lucja said.

'I guess so,' Dion agreed.

I settled my head on my paws, relieved. We'd started this adventure as a family, I intended to make sure we finished it as one too. I'd do anything to bring my sister home safely. Even if it meant another nightmare flight in the hold of a plane, and 10 days in quarantine.

That was just how much I loved Lara.

Chapter
Fourteen

I knew Ben had joked that the shop needed customers, but it wasn't until the next day that I realized quite how desperate things were.

We ate breakfast together in the small kitchen on the shop floor, before he flipped over the sign on the door to 'open'. I took up my station on the armchair to watch for likely-looking shoppers. After a while, I decided that any such shoppers probably wouldn't mind if I had a small nap.

When I awoke, Ben was sipping a cup of coffee and reading a book with a magnifying glass on the cover. 'You didn't miss anything much,' he said, noticing I was awake. 'Well, except my predictions on *Whodunit*. I'm almost certain it was the fishmonger.'

My ears pricked up at the word 'fish' and Ben rolled his eyes before putting down his book. 'Hungry again, huh?'

I led the way into the kitchen and waited for my sardines. It wasn't like he was doing anything else important, anyway.

In the end it was gone lunchtime before the bell on the shop door rang even once, and even then, it was just someone looking for directions. As they left again, Ben looked at me and shrugged. 'The Saturday rush,' he said, wryly. 'It's just this hectic every week.'

I stretched out on my chair, thinking hard as I prepared for action. This wouldn't do at all. What was the point of Ben having all these books if no one wanted to buy them? His shop might be a bit dusty and scruffy, but it was also welcoming and comfortable. People just needed to be persuaded to give it a chance, then I was sure they would love it. Just like I did. Ben had given *me* a chance – and some sardines – after all. Now he needed customers to give him the same opportunity to show them how great he – and his shop – really were.

Clearly, the man needed my help – and my irresistible fluff appeal.

Suddenly, I knew just what I needed to do to help him.

The day was bright and sunny, so I meowed patiently at the door until Ben opened it for me, then proceeded to stretch myself out on the front step in the sunshine. It didn't take long until the first casual shopper paused to pet me.

She was an older woman and the man with her – I assumed to be her husband – rolled his eyes as she stopped by my step. With a wide smile, she crouched down beside me and reached out to pet my fur.

'Moira, is there a cat in the whole of Australia that you won't stop to stroke?' the man asked.

'Possibly, but I've not met them yet,' she admitted, unapologetically. 'Besides, look at her, Stan. She's such a beauty!'

I preened at that, just a little – it's always nice to be appreciated.

'Well, if you're going to be here a while, I might as well have a poke around,' Stan said, stepping over me and pushing open the door to the bookshop.

'Good idea, dear,' Moira said absently. 'You like a good book to read.'

'Gives me something to do while you're befriending the entire cat population of New South Wales,' he muttered.

I rolled onto my back to encourage Moira to rub my tummy. No need to rush Stan in his book perusal now, was there? The longer he stayed, the more likely he was to buy lots of books, I figured.

By the time Moira had had her fill of my marvellously fluffy fur, Stan had bought three books, and promised to return to buy more when he'd finished them. 'It's hard to find a good second-hand bookshop these days,' he told Ben, when he opened the door for him. 'I'll definitely be back.'

'Me too,' Moira added, as she straightened up. 'Next time maybe I'll even look at the books. But to be honest, it'll mostly be to see this beauty. What's her name?'

'Elizabeth,' Ben replied, looking confused at all the attention.

'You should put her picture in the window,' Moira told him. 'She'll pull in plenty of customers, for sure!' Then she squinted at the windows. 'Might want to clean them first, though.'

'Right,' said Ben. 'I'll, uh, think about that. Thank you.'

Stan and Moira wandered off again, bickering amiably as they went.

Ben looked down at me: 'Sardines?'

I got to my feet and padded through the open door. It was hard work, being a living advertisement.

After my sardine break, I resumed my place on the front step, where I was quickly discovered by a family of five. The two younger kids and the dad stayed outside to pet me, while the eldest child and the mum explored the shop – and left with a bag full of purchases.

'Second-hand book shops are fantastic for us,' the mum explained, as she emerged with a bulging bag. 'I can buy some-thing for everyone without breaking the bank!'

The eldest daughter came running out behind her, another book in her hand. 'Mum! Can I have this one too? It'll be really useful for school …'

Mum looked doubtfully at the garish yellow, pink and green cover, but took it anyway. 'One more, apparently. I can't say no to them reading, you see.'

'Absolutely not,' Ben agreed. 'I'll just ring it up for you.'

Of course, that was when the two youngest decided to explore the shop, rampaging through the stacks until they found the brightly coloured cushioned area with the selection of children's books, and a few small toys to play with. Their dad sat in my armchair and read them picture books for a little longer, before they were all ready to leave. It was nice to see the shop full of life, with people enjoying the books.

That said, it was much more peaceful once they'd left.

'Come back again soon,' Ben said, as he waved them goodbye.

'We will!'

Ben propped the door open with a small stack of hardbacks. 'Since it's such a nice day,' he explained. Then he placed my water bowl on the step for me and took a seat in my armchair by the window, watching for our next customers.

I purred happily to myself. It was no longer a question of *if* Ben would get any more customers today. With me there to drum up trade, it was just a matter of time.

Next up was a young couple – two lovely girls looking for set texts for their university courses, apparently.

'I never even realized this place was here,' one of them said, as Ben rang up their purchases. 'I guess because it doesn't look like much from the outside, does it?'

'Right.' Ben pulled a face at the filthy windows.

'I'll have to come back and look for something to read for fun soon. Once I get this assignment out of the way, anyway,' the girl added.

'What made you notice it today?' Ben asked, curiously. I wasn't at all curious, I already knew the answer – it was obvious to anyone with eyes and a love of cats. But apparently, Ben was still too surprised at the sudden surge in custom to have realized it.

'Your cat!' The other girl giggled. 'Abbey has *such* a thing about Ragdolls. We're going to get one together when we move out of halls.'

They headed off together into the fading sun, happy and in love and loaded down with books. Just as they should be.

'I can't decide if you're a good-luck charm, or if I'm going to end up spending all the money you make me on sardines,' said Ben, once we were alone again. 'But I'm just going to go with it for now.'

By the time he flipped the sign over to 'closed' that evening, I'd counted a full 17 customers that had come through the door and bought books. Ben said it was the best day's business he'd had since opening the shop, six years before, which I figured said a lot about how badly he'd been doing before I got there.

Life carried on the same way for the next few days. Ben and I got our routines in sync pretty quickly: I brought in the customers, he provided the food. Soon, word started getting around, and more people showed up at the shop just to buy books, rather than to see me. I supposed that was probably a good thing.

'You can't buy word-of-mouth publicity,' Ben said, shaking his head as another customer left. The woman had bought three books, and said her friend Moira had told her to stop by. 'This is incredible, this is what I've been waiting for, ever since we opened.' He smiled down at me. 'You're definitely worth the sardines, Your Majesty.'

Well, I could have told him that.

On the fourth day – and after Moira had been back herself to look at the books – Ben filled a bucket with warm, soapy water, grabbed a sponge, and put both things on the pavement outside the shop. He sighed, and looked in at me on the armchair.

'I don't suppose that fluffy tail of yours is any good for cleaning windows, is it?' he asked.

I didn't dignify that with an answer.

It took Ben most of the day to clean the tall wide windows of the shop, inside and out – especially since he had to keep stopping and drying off his hands to help customers. I gave him moral support throughout by watching from my favourite sunny spot on the front step, inspecting his progress periodically whenever I needed to stretch my legs, and reminding him when it was time to take a break and feed me.

'You're a big help,' Ben said, as I tucked into another bowl of sardines. I think he was being what Mum calls sarcastic. But even he had to admit that the shop looked much brighter and welcoming once the windows were clean. We stood together out on the pavement in the fading sunlight at the end of the day and looked on at our work.

'Only thing is, I'm going to have to redo the window displays now,' he said, with a sigh. But he didn't sound too disappointed about it. In fact, he sounded almost excited.

I took that as a good sign.

Ben even put a poster with a picture of me on it in the front window, with a sign he told me said, '*Come in and meet Elizabeth, the bookshop cat*'. 'That way, people will know you're here, even if it's raining or cold, and you'd rather be on your armchair.'

That sounded like a sensible idea to me. It was very demanding being a public figure, it turned out. I needed to look after myself, or my fur might get thin and ratty.

There was one very odd moment that first week, though. It was a cool, grey morning, just after we'd opened. I was curled up in my armchair while Ben sipped his coffee, reading the headlines from the daily paper to me (even though I had no idea who any of the people he was talking about were). Normally, our customers didn't come in until a little later in the morning, so we tended to take the early hours for ourselves, enjoying the peace of the shop without any customers. Ben joked sometimes that he never expected to long for the quiet of an empty shop, back when that was all he ever had!

Still, when the shop door opened, we assumed it was someone there to choose a book – it did feel like just the day for snuggling up and reading a good one, Ben had said when he first came down that morning. But instead, the lady skipped all the stacks of books, weaving her way through them, and went straight to the counter.

'I'd like to see your cat, please,' she said, giving Ben a hard stare. Apparently, in her efforts to avoid knocking over any of the book towers, she'd missed me completely on her way past the armchair.

'My cat?' Ben smiled easily, the way he always did with new customers. 'You're not the first person to ask that. She's on the armchair behind you.'

He was right. It wasn't the wanting to see me part that was odd – that happened all the time, especially since Ben put the photo in the window. It was what happened next that was *really* strange.

'You say her name is Elizabeth?' she asked, as she scrutinized me. She didn't stroke me or pet me or make a fuss of me, like all the other customers did: she just *looked* at me. I curled up tighter into a ball at the back of the armchair. I have no problem with being admired, but being studied always makes me feel like I'm at the vet's surgery.

Ben obviously picked up on my unease, as he moved forward to stand between me and the woman.

'Yes,' he said, defensively. 'Elizabeth has been with me for years, eating me out of sardines and home.'

I glanced up at him at the lie. Was he just protecting me from the intimidating lady, or was he truly scared that someone was going to come and claim me, take me away? I suppose he had no idea where I'd come from, or if I had a family out searching to bring me home. And I guess he didn't want to lose me now, not when I was such a big draw for the bookshop.

But he needn't have worried. I knew that Mum and Dad and Gobi would be far too busy to miss me. They had TV interviews and book tours to do, after all, just the three of them. There was nothing a fluffy cat like me could add to their lives, no way I could help them – not like I was helping people here in Australia.

And even if my microchip now said that I belonged to Jennifer, she knew I wasn't really her cat either. I didn't think she'd come searching for me, or try and claim me. In fact, I was almost certain she'd trust that the universe had another job for me, or something. That it was fate that I leave her.

Actually, maybe she was right on that one, now I thought about it. Weird, hey?

Anyway, the point was, I was a free agent, I could come and go as I wanted. It just so happened that what I wanted right now was a comfortable armchair surrounded by books, a steady stream of customers to admire me, and sardines on demand, that was all.

'Huh.' The woman stood up straight again, since she couldn't really see me past Ben, anyway. 'It's funny, she looks just like a cat I saw a photo of on telly recently. Her owners had launched some sort of international search for her.'

Lucky cat, I thought. *Mine probably hadn't even noticed I'd gone.* They'd certainly never start the sort of campaign they had to find Gobi, when she was lost.

'I think most Ragdoll cats look quite alike, really,' said Ben. The woman didn't seem to notice the nerves in his voice, but I did – he *really* didn't want to lose me. And he was totally wrong, anyway: I was unique. Ragdolls only looked the same to people who weren't paying attention. Like my family, and Jennifer, when Cleo and I swapped places.

Eventually the woman left, apparently satisfied I wasn't the cat she was looking for. Ben took the poster down from the window after that, which was a shame, as I liked sitting on my armchair and waiting for people to come and pet me – it felt a bit like a throne.

Life went back to normal. In fact, the intimidating woman's visit was the only strange thing to happen at the bookshop, really. At least, until the day that Gareth arrived.

Chapter
Fifteen

The day Gareth arrived started off much like all the others. Ben had given me breakfast while he made himself coffee, then we'd settled companionably by the door – me in the rays of morning sunshine falling on my armchair, him reading the paper behind the counter – and waited for our first customers.

And probably the day would have carried on like all the others, if I hadn't spotted a teenage boy behaving in a very suspicious manner as he passed the shop.

He was shorter than Ben, gangly and awkward, wearing a dark hooded top and grubby jeans and trainers. His dark hair flopped over onto his forehead under the hood, and his gaze jolted around everywhere, as if afraid he was being followed.

Hmm. Definitely not the normal sort of customer we got around here. My curiosity was piqued.

Ben didn't seem to see him – or if he did, he ignored him. But it was a rare slow day and I was curious, so I stood up, stretched, and followed the teenager as he moved away from the front door.

Just as well I did. As I watched, the boy checked over his shoulder, then ducked behind the bookshop, into the alley usually only frequented by mice and rats. (I'd mostly let them be. They didn't taste as good as sardines, and I was sure that Ben appreciated that my value to him and the shop was measured in customers, rather than dead rodents.) What on earth could he be looking for, back there?

I followed him to find out, of course, treading daintily over the damp patches and scattered rubbish. The boy was too busy peering back around the wall of the shop to notice me at first, so I meowed. Loudly.

I'm not used to being ignored.

He looked down, his eyes going wide as he spotted me. 'Shush!' he hissed.

I meowed again, mostly to be contrary. I didn't like this stranger loitering around my shop, and I didn't much like being told to be quiet, either.

The boy's expression turned a little panicked. Was he scared of cats or something? Clearly, he just needed to get to know us to love us. Except that would mean him hanging around my shop and, right then, I was perfectly happy to chase him off so Ben and I could go back to our normal, peaceful existence.

He flapped his hands towards me, ineffectually. 'Go on, shoo! Get out of here, you stupid cat, you'll give me away!'

I ignored him. Apart from anything else, how could he possibly be referring to me if he was using the phrase 'stupid cat'?

He peered around the wall again. I meowed again, hoping it would encourage him to talk. This was normally the point in the proceedings where humans found themselves explaining themselves to me, telling me all about what was going on in their lives and what their problems were, you see. That was how it had worked with Jennifer, Anya and Ben, anyway. I was fully expecting the boy at any moment to turn around, sigh, and then tell me everything. But apparently he hadn't got that instruction, because he just continued to glare at me.

Not very informative.

'Gareth? Gareth?' A woman's voice floated around from the street. From the way the boy's eyes widened even further –

something I hadn't been sure was possible until then – I guessed that *he* was Gareth.

'Please,' he whispered to me, 'please don't give me away.'

I stared back, promising nothing.

It wasn't quite a full confession, but at least it was an acknowledgement that he had a problem he needed help solving. I started looking at him differently – not so much as someone loitering around my shop and ruining a peaceful morning, but as another human who needed a cat to sort their lives out for them, maybe. But first, I had a lot of questions that needed answering. What was he doing here? And who was he hiding from, and why? Until I had answers to those questions, I definitely wasn't picking sides. Maybe the woman calling for him was the person who *really* needed help. But I couldn't be sure.

Which meant I couldn't do anything to give away his hiding place either, I realized. After all, he might be hiding for a very good reason. Gareth could just be the next person I needed to help, now I'd got Ben and his shop sorted out nicely – or he might be the one causing someone else's problems. I'd just have to watch and see what happened next to find out.

'Gareth?' Another call, closer this time, echoed into the alleyway.

Gareth's head jerked from side to side as he looked around him, then he dove into the doorway at the back of the shop, thudding against the back door as he tried to hide himself. I followed, to check how well he could be seen. The door itself was set back into the wall with a step up from the alleyway, which was where Gareth had curled himself up. His dark clothing blended surprisingly well against the wood of the door, and with his hood over his head, it was hard to tell from the alleyway that there was even a human in there at all.

Satisfied that he was suitably hidden from view of whoever was hunting for him, I sauntered around to the front of the shop to find out what was happening there. Maybe the person looking for Gareth might give me more answers than he had – that would be a help.

'Gareth? Oh …' The woman who had been calling looked to be about Ben's age, but more nicely dressed by far. Her camel coloured jacket was neatly belted at the waist and, even if it didn't look new, it was clean. Her dark blonde hair fell about her shoulders in waves, and she held her body stiffly, as if forcing it to stay upright.

In many ways, she was the opposite of scruffy, relaxed Ben. Still, she looked sad in the same way he did, and her shoulders fell as she saw me appear from behind the shop. The hope disappeared from her eyes, and that sad feeling grew, just from being nearer to her.

'Is everything okay out here?' Ben asked, from the shop doorway. He sounded amiable enough, but his brown eyes were wary. Of the woman? She didn't seem very threatening. Or had he seen more of what was happening than I'd thought? Did he know Gareth was hidden behind his shop right now? I wasn't sure.

The woman turned to face him, a sad smile on her face. 'I'm sorry, I thought I saw … I thought I saw my son.' The last word turned into a sob, and she brought her hands up to her pale face to hide her tears.

Oh, Gareth! I had a feeling he might have got himself – and his mother – into the sort of mess that even *I* couldn't solve on my own. But I knew that I wanted to try and help.

But first we needed to stop the woman from crying.

Ben looked at me, I looked at him. I sensed that this situation couldn't be fixed with sardines, which meant we were both at a total loss for what to do. If she was sitting down I could curl up in her lap and purr comfortingly. But as it was …

Luckily, Ben rose to the occasion.

'Why don't you come in for a cup of tea?' he suggested. 'That always helps me when I'm bothered about something. I've got breakfast or herbal. Or coffee, if you'd prefer. And there's probably some biscuits somewhere. Elizabeth here might even let you share her armchair.'

I would! Because then I could do the purring comfortingly thing, and that would definitely help.

The woman sniffed. 'That would be very kind, thank you. I'm Pollie, by the way.' She held out a hand to him, which he stared at for a long moment before shaking. As much as Ben had grown used to having lots of customers in his shop, I suspected he still wasn't all that comfortable with new people who needed anything besides books.

'Ben.' He gave her an anxious sort of smile as she made her way past him into the shop. 'And this is Elizabeth.'

'You said.' Pollie returned the smile with one of her own – still watery, but genuine, at least.

'Did I? Right. So, um … Tea?'

He really *was* nervous. I took another look at Pollie. Willowy, dark blonde hair past her shoulders, big sad blue eyes, nice dress under that camel jacket. She was quite pretty, I supposed, in a miserable kind of way. Maybe Ben sensed a kindred spirit.

Hmm. Maybe my job with Ben didn't stop at drumming up more business for his bookshop after all. Perhaps he needed more companionship than just customers. Maybe he needed a friend, just like Anya had.

But first, we needed to figure out what was going on with Gareth and Pollie, and how we could help them. Because I was definitely going to need Ben's help for that. And who knew? Maybe both problems would work themselves out, together with a little help from yours truly.

I wondered what Gareth was doing now. I wanted to go and check, but right then it seemed like Pollie needed me more. Besides, if I left now, I'd miss out on hearing the story of what was going on. And without that information, how would I know who to help first? I was pretty sure that Pollie had to be Gareth's mum – that only made sense, right? But in that case, why was he hiding from her? And should we be helping her find him or him to keep hiding?

Pollie took a seat in the armchair, and I curled up in her lap. I'm a calming presence and it's hard to be unhappy when you have a cat snuggling you.

Ben bustled around the kitchen making tea – and knocking a few things over, by the sounds of things – then came back to join us. I was half hoping he'd bring me a snack too, but apparently, I'd have to wait. Clearly, *Pollie* was more in need of his care and attention than I was right then.

'You're looking for your son?' he asked, as he handed her a mug – the one with elephants on, I noticed approvingly. It definitely had less chips and stains than some of the other ones I'd seen him use. He was trying to impress her. (*I'd* be more impressed if he'd brought out the sardines too.)

'Gareth.' Pollie took a sip of the tea. I sat smugly on her lap. I knew it, Pollie was Gareth's mum! It all made perfect sense.

Well, apart from the bit where he was hiding from her. I still hadn't figured that part out yet.

'He's fifteen,' Pollie went on. 'He … he ran away from home three days ago and I've just been frantic ever since I realized he was gone. Everyone is looking for him – the police, my friends, the school, everyone. But there's been no sign anywhere. Not at his friends' houses, not any of the places I know they hang out. He left a note telling me he was sorry and not to look for him. But how can I not search? He's my only child. I've looked everywhere and found nothing. But then I came around the corner into this street and I could have *sworn* that I saw him.'

'He didn't come in here, I'm afraid,' Ben said. I shuffled a little awkwardly on Pollie's lap. If I hadn't come out when I did, she might have made it into the alleyway and found him there, if she'd looked long and hard enough. And I got the feeling that Pollie would have searched that whole alley if there was even the smallest chance of her son being there somewhere.

Had I made the wrong choice? Should I have led her round there to find him? She seemed so upset … But I still didn't know why Gareth had run away in the first place.

I wished I could head back out to the alley and ask him – well, meow until he caved and told me. I couldn't imagine he was still out there, though. He'd have run again, as soon as he realized his mum had been distracted; he wouldn't want to risk her finding him.

Which meant he could be anywhere by now.

How could I help either of them if I didn't even know where Gareth was?

'To be honest, it's possible I was just hallucinating him,' Pollie admitted. 'I haven't slept since he left, I've been so worried …'

'I'm sure,' Ben said, soothingly. 'It must be terrifying, not knowing where he is.'

She nodded, stifling another little sob.

Ben looked alarmed. He didn't seem to do well with tears. 'But you know, sometimes boys, they don't think through the consequences of their actions. Maybe he's already realized he made the wrong choice, and is trying to figure out a way to come back right now.'

Pollie looked up, her eyes bright with hope. 'Do you think so?'

I didn't – I'd seen how carefully Gareth had hidden himself in that doorway.

'What do I know?' Ben shrugged, and gave her a self-deprecating smile. 'But I do hope he comes home for you soon. I'm sure he must be missing you too.'

Pollie stayed a little while longer, sipping tea and talking with Ben about the terrors of raising teenagers. It sounded pretty awful, to be honest. I was almost surprised that she wanted Gareth back. From what they said, it seemed that teenagers just slept a lot and demanded food at all hours.

Really, you might as well just get a cat – we smell less too.

'For someone who's never had kids, you seem to know a lot about how they think,' Pollie said, as she put down her empty cup and prepared to leave.

Ben looked down at his feet with a shy smile. 'I read a lot. And I like getting inside characters' heads, understanding how their brains work. I guess it's just a bit like that.'

'Perhaps. And thank you, just talking about Gareth has helped. And I mean it – whether it's the books or not, you really do seem to have a knack for understanding teenage boys.'

Ben's smile grew wider as he looked at her from under his eyelashes. 'Maybe I just never grew up myself.'

'Maybe.' Pollie flashed him a smile in return – the first I'd seen since she appeared outside our shop.

'Let me know if – I mean, *when* – he comes home?' Ben asked, and Pollie nodded, her smile fading.

'Of course. I just hope it's soon.' She looked away. 'I'm not sure how much longer I can go on like this.'

'I'm sure it will be soon,' Ben said, reassuringly. 'And in the meantime, if you need anything, or want to talk some more, I'm here.' He grabbed a business card for the bookshop from the cash desk and handed it to her. 'You should give me your number, too – in case I spot him around here again.'

'Of course.' Pollie picked up another card and a pen, and scribbled some numbers on the back. Then she pulled a sheet of paper out of her bag. 'I've been putting these up all over town. It has his photo on it – the best one I could find, anyway. He hates having his photo taken. Anyway, you should take it so you know what he looks like.'

Ben took the piece of paper from her, studying it carefully as if committing it to memory. 'I'll put it up in the window here, too.'

Oh, so *Gareth* got his photo on the window, but not me? How fair was that?

Pollie seemed pleased, though. 'Why are you being so nice to me?' she asked, stopping halfway through putting on her jacket. 'You don't even know me. For all you know, I might have driven my son away by being the world's worst mother.'

'I doubt it. But even if you did, right now *you* need help,' Ben said, simply. 'I always think the world would be a better place if we helped more and judged less.'

Pollie looked at him with wide eyes, her jacket forgotten. 'I suppose it would.'

The moment stretched out, the two of them just watching each other, until I couldn't bear it any more. Meowing loudly, I brushed up against Pollie's legs and batted her jacket with my paw, until she remembered what she was supposed to be doing.

Honestly, these humans! No focus, that was their problem.

Ben waited on the step outside the front door to wave her goodbye, but a nagging feeling led me to potter back around the side of the shop and into the alley again. Just in case.

And there, still sat in the back doorway, was Gareth – he *hadn't* run after all.

Why? What did that mean? I wondered. *Maybe Ben would know.* I wished I could ask him.

Gareth sniffed, and I realized he was crying. Maybe he wanted to go home and didn't know how? Except his mum was right there, so what was stopping him? I didn't understand.

Something tugged at my heart at that thought. A sense that maybe he wasn't the only one lost and confused.

I ignored it.

He might have called me a stupid cat, but that didn't mean I wanted Gareth to have to live out his days in the back alley of a second-hand bookshop. Besides, his mum obviously missed him. If no one else was going to fix this situation, I would have to figure out how to do it on my own, after all.

I was just about to race back around to the front of the shop to try and get Pollie's attention and lead her back here to Gareth when the back door to the shop opened, and Ben looked out.

He looked down at Gareth, raised his eyebrows and said, 'I think you'd better come inside, don't you?'

Chapter
Sixteen

Gareth sat at the tiny table in the kitchen, looking at his grubby hands and twitching nervously. Ben, calmer than I'd ever seen him – and definitely calmer than he had been when Pollie was sat in the shop, crying – set about making a sandwich from whatever was left in the fridge, and poured the boy a large glass of water. He placed both things in front of Gareth, then eased himself into the chair opposite.

Gareth took one long look at the sandwich, then at Ben, and dove in, ripping into the food faster than I go through a bowl of prawns. (I really wished I could have some prawns! I understood Ben's need to nurture Gareth and Pollie, but there were others starving here, too, didn't he realize?)

'Been a while since your last meal, huh?' Ben asked. But Gareth didn't stop eating to answer, he just nodded.

I had sat myself at Gareth's feet in case there were any scraps, but that didn't look at all likely. Finally noticing me, Ben got up again and fixed me a bowl of sardines.

That's the sort of human all pets need: one who notices the important things in life. Eventually.

'I'm Ben, by the way. And this is Elizabeth,' he told Gareth, motioning to me with the tin of sardines. 'She's the one who spotted you. I only put it together when she went back out to the alley after your mum left.'

I should have known that this whole rescue was down to me. Honestly, humans! How did they ever cope without us?

Gareth froze at the mention of his mother. 'Did Mum go back home?'

'Yes. For now.' Ben had forgotten about the sardines, leaving them on the counter. Reasoning that he wouldn't want me to starve, I hopped up and helped myself.

'Are you going to tell her that I'm here?' When he looked up, from my vantage point on the counter, I could see that Gareth's eyes were wide, white all the way around the irises. He looked terrified. But what was he so scared of? It couldn't be *Pollie*, could it? She'd seemed nice. Sad, but kind. Like Ben.

Ben sat down again, eyeing Gareth carefully. 'That depends.'

'On what?' he asked.

'On why you ran away in the first place.' Resting his forearms on the table, Ben leaned forward, his hands clasped together as he spoke to the boy. His eyes and his tone were understanding – no shouting, no demanding explanations, just patient understanding. 'I know what it's like to have to get out of a place. To leave and not look back, because it was better to be alone and scared than to be there with other people and terrified. So, if you tell me you can't go back because you're afraid for your life or your mind, I will help you. If you tell me you're a victim of abuse or bullying or *anything* close to that, I will get you out. So, tell me, is that why you can't go home? Is that why you ran?'

I'd never heard Ben sound so serious. *I know what it's like*, he'd said. How did he know? I'd never imagined that he had a life even, before he became the tatty owner of a tatty bookshop. But obviously he had.

Suddenly, I wanted to learn more about Ben's life. He'd never talked about anything beyond the bookshop in the weeks I'd been staying with him. I wondered if tonight he would.

Gareth stared at Ben for a long moment. Then he looked down at his sandwich and shook his head. He looked a little ashamed, I thought. But Ben wasn't going to let him get away with a shake of the head. With Pollie, he'd just listened – let her pour out all her fears, all her memories of Gareth as a little boy, all her confusion about what had gone wrong. But with Gareth, he was taking charge of the conversation – and he expected answers. He wouldn't lose his temper, but he would wait Gareth out with his unending patience. It was sort of like the way I demanded food – I didn't scratch or bite, I just waited very close, meowing occasionally, until someone gave in and fed me.

Sometimes I thought Ben would have made a good cat.

'Then why, Gareth?' he pressed, leaning a little further forward, 'why did you run away?'

'You're going to think it's stupid,' Gareth mumbled. He wasn't looking up, so he probably didn't see the smile Ben stifled.

'Maybe,' Ben allowed. 'But what seems stupid at first glance to one person can be deadly serious to another. Like I said to your mum when she told me her side of this story, in this world we need to judge less and listen more. So, just tell me. I promise to listen, not laugh, or judge. I only want to help you. You *and* your mum, if I can, that's all.'

Gareth stared up at him for a long moment, like he was trying to figure out if Ben was for real. If he really believed all that stuff about helping.

I knew he did, though. Because while I'd been helping him, I realized suddenly that he'd been helping me, too. I'd been so busy focussing on all the good *I* was doing at the bookshop, it had taken me a while to notice everything *Ben* did.

He'd never tried to find out where I came from, or asked for anything more than my company in the shop. But he'd fed me and sheltered me and let me make my home there. He'd taken me in when I had nowhere else to go.

All this time, I'd thought that help only went one way. That I was the one doing the helping, getting him new customers. I never really stopped to think about how much I got in return: food, shelter – and most of all, love.

I hoped Gareth was as lucky – and as trusting – as I'd been. If so, I thought Ben could be the best friend he'd ever found.

'It's just … It's always been just me and Mum at home, you see,' Gareth said, finally, fidgeting with the ends of his sleeves as he spoke. 'Dad was never even in the picture, so it was always just the two of us. And I was her everything, she used to say. The most important thing in the world to her.'

'I definitely got that impression when we spoke,' Ben said, softly.

'And that's great and all. I mean, I love her too! Of course, I do. But being the most important thing in the world for her … it meant she pinned all her hopes and dreams on me. Always wanted me to be the best – well, try my hardest, anyway, she said.'

'I see.' Ben didn't say anything more, just waited for Gareth to fill in the silence. It was a clever technique, actually. I figured it was sort of like why people talk to cats so much. When the other person in the room isn't saying anything, people feel obliged to make up for them.

It worked, anyway. Now he'd started, the words came spilling out of Gareth like water from the kitchen tap, like he couldn't stop them if he tried.

'She just always expected so much! I couldn't live up to it, you know? Too much pressure. And then …' He looked down at the table, and ran his hand through his greasy hair.

I wondered if he was going to finish that sandwich. The sardines were nice, but lunch had been a really long time ago, and it was practically suppertime by now.

'I got into trouble at school,' Gareth went on. 'Like, really bad trouble, not just I forgot my homework a few times. They suspended me even. And I knew that if I went home, my mum would just be so … not even angry, just disappointed. Like, devastated that her son had been suspended, humiliated by me. And I just couldn't do that to her. I was walking home from school and I just … I realized I just wanted to keep walking. I knew Mum would still be at work, so I snuck back into the house to grab a few things and leave her a note, then I just walked out. And I never went back.'

'What did you do to get suspended?' Ben asked. I was glad, because I wanted to know, too. (I know what they say about cats and curiosity, but to be honest, I don't buy it. Besides, if it came to that, at least I'd die satisfied.)

'There was this new boy, right?' Gareth looked up and met Ben's gaze. I could see a sort of pleading in his eyes, a hope that Ben would keep understanding. That he'd get it. 'And some of the other guys in my year were teasing him. No, not teasing, it was worse than that.'

'Bullying?' Ben's expression turned sour. I could tell he understood *completely*.

'Yeah. They wouldn't call it that, though – they said they were just having a laugh.'

'You didn't agree?' Ben guessed.

Gareth shook his head. 'I went along with it to start with. You know, you do, don't you? To keep them from starting in on you instead. But then it just didn't feel right so I told them to stop.' He pulled the cuffs of his hooded top over the ends of his hands completely, fisting his fingers inside them.

I thought about Anya and the Mean Girls at her school. I thought about the alley cats and the sandwich and the bin. And suddenly I liked Gareth a whole lot more. Maybe he had run away and upset his mum, and maybe he was grubby and a bit smelly and sulky. But he'd done good things too – he'd tried to help another person.

I'd been grubby and sulky and even smelly at times too. I couldn't really hold it against him.

My supper finished, I jumped down from the counter onto Gareth's lap to offer my best purring services. He started with surprise, but soon enough he was stroking my fluffy fur like everyone else did.

Seriously. I was basically a stress-relief toy at this point. So much better than those squishy globes or baseballs Dad brought back from trips sometimes.

'They didn't listen to me,' Gareth went on, and I could tell from his haunted expression that he was reliving the moment in his head. 'They just kept on taunting the new guy, grabbing his stuff and flinging it around, and then they starting grabbing him. I couldn't watch it and not do anything. So I made them stop.'

'You got suspended for fighting,' Ben summarised. 'And the school didn't care that you were doing it for all the right reasons.'

'Basically, yeah.' Gareth gave him a small, surprised smile. 'You get it.'

'They never do,' Ben said. 'Schools, authority figures … sometimes they're too tied up in their own problems to even *notice* the context of what we do. Which means it ends up that it's always more about rules than people, in my experience. You were trying to help – maybe not the best way or the right way, because you seldom solve anything with your fists – but you were trying to do the right thing. That might not mean much to the rule-makers, but it means a lot to me.'

'Did you get into a lot of fights at school?' Gareth asked, curiously. He looked younger, now his secrets were out. More vulnerable. Like a kitten who didn't know how to find the food bowl yet.

Ben had a small, embarrassed smile on his face. I tried to imagine him fighting, and failed. He just wasn't the violent sort, more the curling-up-with-a-book-and-a-cat sort. Which is why his answer surprised me so much.

'One or two,' he admitted. 'But most of my fighting happened at home. See, in my case, it was my stepfather hitting my mother, rather than other boys at school. But in the end, it's all the same thing – the insecure bullies picking on someone smaller and weaker than them.'

'What happened?' Gareth asked, his eyes wide. 'With your stepdad, I mean?'

Ben tilted his chair back, staring at the ceiling as he spoke.

'When I finally got big enough, strong enough, I hit him back. I thought I could save my mum, get her out of there, but …' he shook his head. 'She didn't want to go, said she still loved him. So, I left. If I'd stayed, I don't like to think what he'd have done to me.'

'You never went home?'

Ben let his chair legs fall to the ground, so his eyes were level with Gareth's again. 'I never went home.'

They stared at each other in silence for a long moment. I watched them, motionless on Gareth's lap, just able to see Ben over the edge of the table. But in the still and quiet of the room, my mind was spinning and shouting.

They'd both left home out of fear – and so had I, in a way. I'd been so scared of not being as good as Gobi, as adventurous as Gobi, as important as Gobi – as *loved* as Gobi – I'd come all the way to the other side of the world to prove myself. To prove to my family how much they'd miss me. But it hadn't worked. After all, what was I really proving? And who was I proving it to, with my family thousands and thousands of miles away, unaware of my adventures?

I wasn't sure what the point of it all was any more. No, that wasn't true. My reasons might have changed, but I knew why I was here – why I'd needed to get out into the world, alone.

It wasn't just to see new things or meet new people. It wasn't about how far I'd travelled or the experiences I'd had. I'd thought that was it, at the start. But I'd learned a lot since then. It was the good that I'd done on the journey that mattered most. That, and the love that I had found on the way.

I *knew* I'd done good things since I'd been in Australia. I felt it inside me, and in the love received from the people I'd helped. I'd seen more of the world than just the view from a window, and I'd learned that it wasn't just the *seeing*, it was the *living*. And it was the animals and people I met along the way that mattered most.

I wasn't the same Lara who'd left Edinburgh – not by a long way. I'd been Cleo and Fortune and Puss and Elizabeth since then, so how could I be? But I knew deep down, in my heart, I was still Lara. Still Dad's baby, still Gobi's sister. Still the indoor cat who chased butterflies in the garden and curled up to sleep with my tail over Gobi's back.

Still the cat who missed her family when they were gone.

I loved all the people I'd met on my adventure, and I'd never regret being part of their lives, but they weren't my family – nobody could take their place.

Then, into the silence, Gareth spoke the words I could hear echoing in my own mind.

'I want to go home,' he said, his voice small and a little lost.

Ben nodded, just once. 'Then I will help you,' he said.

Emptiness filled me, even as a relieved smile spread across Gareth's face.

I want to go home, too, I thought. *But how?*

And most importantly, who was going to help *me*?

 Gobi

Eventually – after more trips to the vet for checks, more paperwork, and a lot of frustration – I was cleared to travel to Australia. I was relieved – I wanted to go and bring Lara home, of course – but also nervous. My last journey in the hold of a plane had been harrowing, and not an experience I'd ever want to repeat, if it wasn't for Lara.

'Are you sure we're doing the right thing?' Dion asked, as they sorted my supplies, ready for the long journey. 'It's not too late to make arrangements for Gobi to stay here in Britain.'

Yes, it was: I was going, and that was that.

I barked to that effect, and Lucja laughed.

'I'm not sure, no,' she admitted. 'But I think Gobi is.'

Too right! I settled down again next to my carrier, to show I was ready to leave when they were.

And so, soon enough, it was time to get back onto the ferry over to France, to catch another plane. Dion and Lucja had decided they didn't want me to travel apart from them any more than necessary, and I agreed (whether they knew it or not). After the ferry, we were flying out from Paris to Australia, via Singapore for a short layover, where I'd be moved from the cabin on one plane to the hold on the other.

At least the part where I'd be in the hold was shorter than the one where I'd be in the cabin. Dion had explained that to me in great detail, while apologizing again for me having to do it. 'Some people, companies and countries just don't understand how important animals are,' he'd told me.

Lucja had hugged us both, then.

Apart from packing and preparing me for the journey, Dion had spent the last week or so on the phone to contacts in Australia, as well as emailing and chatting in forums, trying to make contact with the elusive Jennifer. So far there was no luck, but he said that interest in our story was growing over there, which could only help. The more people who knew about Lara and were on the lookout for her, the better. And now we had more information to share with them than just 'missing Ragdoll cat', which was something.

'I've got a few local TV and radio spots lined up already,' he told Lucja, as they finished packing their suitcases the night before we left for the ferry port. 'That could help us get Jennifer's attention.'

'Or even the attention of someone who knows her or her family,' Lucja added. 'Remember, it only takes one.'

That was our mantra at the moment: it only took one person to see our message at the right time. That one person could contact another and another, until Lara was tracked down, and we could have my sister home again. And if we had to speak to a hundred, a thousand, a million people before we found that one right person, then we would keep on talking.

Or rather, Dion and Lucja would. I just barked, but they said that barking helped too.

'Nearly time to go,' Dion said, as they placed the last items in the bags. I kept remembering how Lara had hidden in the suitcases when-

ever we were preparing to go away before. I missed seeing her furry form jumping out from piles of clothes and shoes.

'She'll be home again soon,' Lucja said, and I knew she was remembering it, too.

We were all on edge, I could feel it.

The airport in Paris – the one where we'd lost Lara – was packed with people the day we flew out to Singapore. We had to push through crowds just to get to the check-in desk, and then the line to get through security snaked back through the terminal. I'd never seen so many people trying to travel at once.

No wonder Cleo had been able to hide in the airport for so long. There were so many people, so many hiding places, that it would be easy for one small cat to stay missing if she didn't want to be found. And that was just in an airport. How much harder would it be to find one cat in a whole country?

I shook my head. I couldn't think I like that. We needed to stay positive, Dion said. We needed to believe that we would find Lara.

Still, the crush of people all around me made us all nervous.

Dion kept me close in my harness, the lead wrapped tight around his fist. Lucja didn't leave his side, either. We were all too aware of how easy it was to get separated in a place like this.

But not this time. This time, we'd be bringing Lara home, not losing anyone else. I had hope.

'Excuse me, but is this Gobi?' A woman stopped us just after the security check, crouching down beside me to make a fuss of me. 'I'd recognise that cute face anywhere!'

She chatted to Dion and Lucja for a while after that, talking about how she'd followed our story, read the book – and how sorry she was to hear about Lara. It seemed that people everywhere were talking about my missing sister. Just not the right ones. Not yet.

Dion gave her a tight smile. 'We're flying out to bring her home, we hope.'

The woman's face lit up. 'Oh! So, you've found her? You know where she is? That's wonderful!'

'We're narrowing it down,' Lucja answered.

'How brilliant!' the woman said, sounding relieved. 'I've been so worried for you. So? Where is she?'

Dion and Lucja shared a look, as if they were finally realizing how impossible all of this was.

'Somewhere in Australia,' Dion admitted, and the woman's face fell. I knew how she felt.

'Somewhere in … right. Well, good luck, I really hope you find her.'

Her tone told me she didn't expect us to. Well, we'd just have to prove her wrong, then. Her and everyone else who thought Lara would never come home.

My sister wouldn't leave me. Not for ever. I had faith in that fact.

We just had to find her. Even Cleo had been found hiding in the airport eventually. How much harder could it really be to find Lara?

I mean, how big was Australia, anyway?

Chapter
Seventeen

Gareth spent the night on the sofa in Ben's flat upstairs, but not before he'd devoured another three sandwiches and half a packet of biscuits. I slept on my armchair, keeping guard over them both by the front door. We'd saved Gareth from the streets, I didn't want to risk anything happening to him now.

That night, I dreamt that Gareth and I were out on the streets together – both homeless and hungry, both with nowhere else to go. Everywhere we went, people threw us out, or automatic doors wouldn't open for us. Alley cats chased us, and trees fell down around us when we raced into a forest to escape them. But through it all, we had each other.

I wondered what Gareth's dreams were like, or whether he was so exhausted and relieved to have a bed for the night (even if it was really a sofa) that he didn't sleep at all.

If he *had* dreamt, he didn't say anything about it when he got up.

The next morning, while Gareth ate two large bowls of cereal in the kitchen, Ben called Pollie and asked her to meet him at the coffee shop down the road. He said he might have some news on Gareth, which sounded like a bit of a lie to me. But I suppose he wanted to keep all Gareth's options open, in case anything went wrong. Or maybe he just didn't want to let Pollie down if Gareth changed his mind between now and then.

'Where are we going?' Gareth put down his spoon as Ben shrugged into his jacket.

'Not *we*,' Ben explained, dropping his wallet and keys into his pockets. '*Me*. I'm going to go and talk to your mum, tell her everything you told me, and prepare the ground, so to speak. Then I'll bring her here so the two of you can make up.'

'What do I do while you're talking to Mum?' Gareth worried at his lower lip with his teeth, as he picked the spoon up again and started weaving it between his fingers somehow.

I guessed he was feeling nervous. But if he was going to jiggle and fidget for the next hour, I'd far rather he went with Ben instead. He was worse than Gobi at not sitting still! How was I supposed to curl up on his lap if he wouldn't stop moving?

Ben grabbed a book from the nearest stack – somehow, they'd penetrated every room in the building, not just the actual shop – and tossed it to him. 'Read a book. Feed Elizabeth. Eat more cereal. I won't be long.'

'But—'

'It's a bookshop, Gareth. I'm sure you can find *something* here to entertain you while I'm gone. If all else fails, you can start alphabetizing the stock.'

And with that, Ben left.

Gareth and I looked at each other. 'I don't suppose you like cereal, huh?' he asked.

I stared in a disapproving manner, which he seemed to understand because he dug around in the cupboard until he found a packet of cat food for me. It wasn't sardines, but it would do. I stood on the counter next to the bowl and supervised him serving it out. Then I tucked in, while he fixed himself a third bowl of cereal.

Once we'd both eaten, we set up guard back at the armchair, watching through the window for Ben and Pollie returning. I tried sitting on Gareth's lap as a calming influence (and for strokes, obviously), but his knees were jiggling too much, so I ended up on the arm of the chair instead.

Gareth gripped the book Ben had given him tightly in his hand, but I could tell he wasn't reading it. I guessed he was thinking about what his mum would say. Whether she'd welcome him home again, after he'd run away like that, without a word.

Suddenly, I realized my tail was swishing, and one of my paws was jiggling too.

I hadn't even considered what *my* mum and dad might be thinking, with me gone. Or Jennifer, for that matter. I'd run away, just like Gareth had. I'd assumed no one would even notice – or if they did, they wouldn't care too much. I'd planned to return, of course – after my grand adventure. But I hadn't given much thought to what I'd be returning to, until I met Gareth.

Would they be mad? Would they refuse to let me back in because they were so angry? Or would they have forgotten me altogether?

I thought of the time my dad and I had our biggest falling-out. I'd bitten him, hard. (In my defence, he'd been trying to brush me at the time, and he *knows* that I can only take that for so long.) He'd been so mad at me, he didn't speak to me for two whole weeks. Eventually Mum stepped in and forced us to make up. Otherwise he might still not be speaking to me.

That was over just one little bite. How cross would he be about me running away to see the world without even saying a goodbye?

And what about Gobi? Would she have taken over my place in the family completely, since I wasn't there to defend it? Maybe she was happy eating *all* the prawns, as well as her stupid dog biscuits that made me sick. She'd be getting all the snuggles and all the attention. She had to be *thrilled* that I wasn't there. Right?

Or … or would they be like Pollie? I hadn't thought of it before, really. But what if they were? What if they were missing me? Scared for me? Unable to sleep because they didn't know where I was?

I almost didn't want to know if that was the case. But I knew I was going to have to find out. My adventure wouldn't be truly complete until I did.

I'd always planned to go home, and I knew now it was almost time. But not until I'd finished my work here, with Ben and Gareth.

I had things I still needed to fix, first. Starting with reconciling Pollie and Gareth, if I could.

Suddenly, with a jolt, Gareth sat up straight, his back rigid, his arm almost knocking me from my perch as he dropped his book. He jerked to his feet, crossing to the window and touching the glass lightly with his fingertips.

I followed his line of vision as he stared out of the window. Ah, of course! There, walking down the street towards us, were Ben and Pollie.

Time to get back to work.

I jumped down from the chair, and waited for Ben to open the door. A sniffly Pollie stepped in – she'd obviously been crying in the coffee shop. (I was glad to have missed that part!) Except then she saw Gareth and burst into floods of tears again.

'Mu-um,' he said, looking awkward at the tears, too. But he stepped towards her all the same, and in an instant she was wrapping her arms tight around him as if she was afraid he might run again if she let go for a moment.

'I'll go put the kettle on,' Ben said, pointedly looking anywhere else. But Pollie wasn't listening – or paying him any attention at all – anyway.

'Oh, my boy! My precious boy! How could you think I'd be mad at you for defending another student?' she asked, between kisses pressed to her son's hair.

Gareth, for his part, took the attention stoically, apart from the mortified look on his face. I pressed against his leg briefly in solidarity, before hopping up onto the counter to be able to watch the action better.

'To be honest, it was the suspension I thought you'd be mad about, not the other stuff.' Gareth gave a little shrug. 'It goes on my permanent record, see. And you always said my permanent record would be what the universities would look at first, so I might have ruined my chances and—'

'Stop right there!' Pollie pulled back, holding him at arm's length, but her hands still firmly grasping his upper arms. I had a feeling she wouldn't be letting him go for a while. 'Let me get one thing straight, first and foremost. Do I want you to go to university? Yes, because I want you to have the chances that I didn't. Do I want you to make a success of your life? Of course, because every mother wants that for their child. But are they the most important things to me? Not at all, not by miles. Okay?'

Gareth bit his lower lip, his eyes suddenly uncertain. 'Then … you're not mad?'

'Mad?' Pollie shook her head and laughed, low and quiet. 'Gareth, I am the *opposite* of mad!'

'Because you're relieved to have me home,' he guessed, sounding on slightly firmer ground with that idea.

But Pollie shook her head. 'Of course, I'm relieved to know you're safe. And I'm crazy mad that you didn't think you could talk to me about this. And I'm so happy I could cry to think you will come home with me tonight.'

That sounded like a lot of emotions to me. Personally, I was happier with 'hungry' or 'full' as my day-to-day emotional range.

'But besides all that, what matters to me most right now is that you understand one very important thing,' Pollie went on.

'What?' Gareth asked, sounding at a complete loss.

She gave him a small smile, and her head tilted a little to the left. Gareth was actually a tiny bit taller than her, I realized, and she almost had to look up into his eyes.

'Do you know what matters to me most about your life and your choices, about the person you grow up to be?'

He shook his head.

'Okay. Then this is what I need you to understand.' She looked him square in the eyes so he couldn't possibly miss her meaning. I found myself watching, rapt, too. 'What I want most in the whole wide world, Gareth, is for you to be happy. I want you to be loved, and loved well. And beyond those things, I wish for you to grow up kind and honest. To be someone who will do the right thing when it matters, whatever the cost. And from what Ben has told me, that's *exactly* the person you were being when you got into that fight. Okay?'

'O-okay.' Gareth gave her a watery smile, and I could see his eyes were gleaming with tears now, too. I blinked quickly. Not that I was affected or anything, it was probably just all the dust in the bookshop.

'So, do you think you can come home now?' Pollie asked.

Gareth threw himself back into her arms, hugging her tightly. 'Yes. Definitely. I missed you, Mum.'

'Oh, my lovely boy!' Pollie said, softly and sweetly. 'I missed you, too.'

Well, that was all right then, I decided. And so, blinking away the last of the dust, I went to go and find Ben in the kitchen, and see about a little snack of something fishy.

Pollie and Gareth joined us in the kitchen, just as I was finishing up my mid-morning snack. They both had red rims around their eyes, but they were smiling too, so I hoped that meant they'd worked things out.

'Everything okay?' Ben asked, looking up from his book. He was sat at the table, one ankle resting on his knee, looking perfectly relaxed – but I'd noticed he hadn't turned a page the whole time I'd been eating.

I think he was as invested in helping people as I was. Especially Pollie.

'Everything's fine.' Pollie wrapped an arm around Gareth's shoulder and pulled him close. 'We've sorted a lot of things out. More talking to do, I'm sure, but we understand each other better now, don't we, Gareth?'

Gareth just nodded. 'Um, I wanted to say, you know. Thanks, and all that.'

Pollie rolled her eyes. 'What my oh-so-eloquent son is trying to say is …' she let go of Gareth, crossed to where Ben had stood up, and hugged him – tightly, from the way Ben's eyes widened. 'We owe you. Big. I don't know what would have happened if you hadn't … I can't even think about it. So, thank you. From the bottom of my heart, thank you.'

'I, uh, was happy to help.' Ben cleared his throat awkwardly.

I sat back on my haunches and watched as he patted Pollie's back lightly, but made no real effort to extricate himself from her enthusiastic hug. In fact, I was pretty sure he *liked* being hugged by Pollie.

Which was interesting.

I'd thought my work here would be done, now that Pollie and Gareth were reunited and had made up. But now I wondered again if there might be one more job for me to do before I left – finding some real companionship for Ben, after I'd gone.

I'd fixed his bookshop – and I was sure that now they'd found it, his new crowd of customers would keep coming without the draw of me being there to pet and play with. But who would keep him company the rest of the time, when I was gone?

I figured Pollie and Gareth were a better choice than most.

I glanced up at Gareth, but the teenager just rolled his eyes, like he was embarrassed by his mum's behaviour. Clearly, if I wanted to get Ben and Pollie together, I was going to have to do it on my own.

Ben started to pull away from the hug, so I dove in to intervene. Winding myself around both their legs in turn, my tail around Ben's ankle while my head brushed against Pollie's calf, I was able to keep them standing close together, if only to avoid stepping on me.

Pollie laughed. 'Looks like someone else wants in on the thank yous!'

Ben stepped carefully backwards, narrowly missing my tail. 'Well, it's probably Elizabeth you should be thanking. She's the one who actually found Gareth after all.'

'Well then, thank you, Elizabeth.' Pollie dropped down to her knees to pet me properly. 'I'll have to stop by with some treats for you soon, won't I? How do you feel about prawns?'

My ears pricked up at the word, and I purred enthusiastically.

Ben laughed. 'I haven't tried her on prawns yet, but I suspect they'll be a hit.'

Pollie straightened and stood. 'That's Elizabeth's thank you sorted, then. But I still owe you one.'

'Oh, no, really, you don't have to—' Ben stuttered, until Gareth interrupted, putting him out of his misery.

'You should take him out for dinner, Mum.' I hopped up onto the counter beside Gareth to show my solidarity with his idea. Looked like the boy had decided to help out after all – good for him!

'What a great idea, Gareth!' Pollie said, still smiling at Ben. 'What about it? Shall we say next Friday night?'

Looking a little shell-shocked, Ben nodded. 'That would be lovely, thank you.'

I purred. Apparently, this was going to be easier than I'd hoped!

Chapter
Eighteen

Friday night seemed to take for ever to arrive – for all of us.

Somehow, in the intervening week, Gareth appeared to have become Ben's unofficial helper at the bookshop. I imagined it was only a matter of time before it became a paid position. Apparently, while he and Pollie had resolved their differences, they still did better with some time apart. Ben said, in one of their chats over sandwiches, that that was a normal teenage thing and besides, with all the extra customers I was bringing in, he needed the extra help. I wasn't sure that was true, but I assumed that Pollie felt better if she knew Gareth was at the shop, rather than out on the streets again. Plus, it was company for Ben.

And I appreciated the compliment anyway.

Mostly, Ben had Gareth shelving books – and incredibly, it seemed like there might actually be some sort of order emerging from the chaos of stacks and piles. He wasn't as welcoming a staff member as I was – he still tended to grunt at customers rather than smile – but he *was* able to operate the till and speak to humans, which I suppose gave him an edge. And there were a small number of teenage girls I'd never seen before who'd started frequenting the shop since he arrived.

I didn't begrudge him the position, anyway. I was leaving, and it was nice to know that there was someone to help Ben build on all the good work I'd done for his shop while I'd been there. I *did* object to him messing with my sleeping space, though. Or, as it was otherwise known, the children's section.

'How did this get here?' I looked up sharply as Gareth, beating the dust from cushions, pulled my copy of *Finding Gobi* out from between them.

'Just toss it on the counter for now,' Ben called back from where he was organizing a box of new arrivals. (Yes, more books, just what the shop needed.)

I watched as the book I'd cuddled every night since I arrived arced its way through the dust motes of the shop air to land neatly on the counter.

'There are loads more books down here,' Gareth groaned. 'I'm going to have to sort them *all* out!'

'We are a bookshop,' Ben said, mildly. 'It's sort of par for the course.'

While they were both distracted by their tasks, I hopped up onto the counter, and tugged my book down with me, dragging it over to my armchair and pushing it underneath with my paw. That way I'd be able to retrieve it again at bedtime, whatever else Gareth did with the children's section.

It wasn't that I *couldn't* sleep without that little reminder of home, I reassured myself, it was just I'd grown used to it. And it was so worn and well-read it actually made a pretty good pillow at this point.

'Why do you even have a kids' section?' Gareth asked, flinging cushions and beanbags about to get to the many books that had fallen or been tossed underneath by wayward toddlers. My book secure, I padded back over to watch him, careful to avoid flying cushions.

'Um, for the children's books?' Ben said, from safely behind the cash desk.

'Yeah, but you don't even *like* kids,' Gareth replied.

Ben frowned. 'What makes you say that?'

Pointing to the sign I'd spotted on my first day, Gareth read out the words I hadn't been able to decipher: '*Any children left unattended will be fed lots of sugar, encouraged to read books beyond their age range, and led to believe in the importance of half-birthday presents to show a parent's love*'.

'Personally, I think that shows I like children a lot more than adults,' Ben said loftily, but I could see him hiding a smile.

It was nice watching the two of them getting on so well together, actually. As much as I hoped things worked out for Ben and Pollie on their date, I hoped just as much that Ben would stay in Gareth's life as a friend, if not a father figure – they were good for each other.

But speaking of the date … Eventually, Friday night arrived, and it was time to focus on Ben's love life, rather than his bookshop.

'Are you seriously wearing *that*?' Gareth asked, sounding incredulous.

I looked up from my snoozing chair in time to see Ben descend the stairs in a brown jacket I hadn't seen him wear before, a dark red shirt, and a brown and red patterned tie. He looked not neat, exactly, but as if he was making an effort. Which I supposed he was.

'What's wrong with it?' Ben looked self-consciously down at himself.

'It's just a bit … brown,' Gareth replied, unhelpfully.

Jumping up onto the shop counter, I took in the full effect of the outfit. Combined with the tan trousers, Ben's brown hair and his chocolate brown eyes, Gareth had a point. In fact, Ben was starting to look like some of those awful tins of cat food I'd had to eat at Anya's.

Not a good look for anybody.

I yowled my opinion, and Ben pulled a face. Obviously, my meaning was clear, even if I hadn't yet mastered human speech.

'Fine. I'll go change,' he said, with a sigh.

Gareth checked his watch. 'No time. Just lose the jacket and the tie, that'll help.' I was pleased to see that, if not actively excited, Gareth certainly didn't seem to mind Ben and Pollie going out together. He was even offering fashion advice – not that I thought *Gareth* was any sort of clothes guru. Even since he'd moved home again and presumably had full access to all his clothes, I'd still never seen him in anything but jeans and a hoodie.

'But what if she wants to go somewhere posh?' Ben asked, nervously. 'You know, one of those restaurants where they won't even *lend* you a tie if you show up without one.'

Gareth rolled his eyes. 'This is my mother, she hasn't had a date in 14 years. You could take her to McDonald's and she'd be thrilled!'

Poor Pollie, she did seem to have had a rough time of it. I hoped *all* their luck was changing now that I'd come into their lives.

'But *she's* taking *me* out,' Ben pointed out, fiddling nervously with the ends of his tie. If he was going to do that all evening, he should *definitely* take it off, I decided. Nervous was not a good look on him. Pollie had fallen (we hoped) for the calm, assured, practical Ben who'd put her family back together, not this brown parcel of nerves.

I hoped Gareth could help him get his act together before he picked Pollie up.

'Even less reason to worry,' Gareth said, easily. 'You'll proba-bly end up with takeout for two back at our place. She's rubbish at deciding where to eat, then when she finally makes her mind up, nowhere has any tables left and we end up back at home. Happens all the time.'

'Right.' A frown creased across Ben's forehead. 'Wait. Did you say *date*?' Apparently, the rest of the conversation had just caught up with him. It seemed that nerves made him slow – not a good sign for the rest of the evening.

It also prompted another eye roll from Gareth. This time I joined it. '*Of course* it's a date, what did you think was going on here?'

'She said a thank you dinner …' Ben trailed off and shrugged. 'I didn't like to presume.'

Gareth shook his head. 'The two of you are worse at this than me – and I'm a 15-year-old guy. At least I've got an excuse for being rubbish at relationships!'

'Oh yes? And what relationships have you been developing with girls – or boys – then?' Ben asked, his lips twitching up in a small smile as the nerves obviously dissipated. He was back on home ground, teasing Gareth about teenage stuff. 'Anything I should tell your mother about?'

'Definitely not,' Gareth replied, firmly. 'And nothing, really … Yet.'

If he'd asked me, I'd have suggested there probably wouldn't be, either, until he washed that hoodie.

'I'll endeavour to improve my social skills before you start needing my advice, then,' Ben said, tugging off his tie and leaving his jacket slung over the back of my armchair. 'Don't wait up, Elizabeth. Gareth, lock up before you leave? And text your mother when you're heading home – you know how she worries.'

'Yes, sir.' Gareth sketched an odd-looking salute, and then Ben was gone, off on his date. He seemed to walk with more purpose and less nerves now the tie and jacket were off, thankfully.

The door swung shut. Gareth stared at it for a long moment, before looking down at me and frowning. 'Is it me, or did that sound like he's planning on sticking around for a while?'

It definitely did. I purred in satisfaction.

Both Ben and Pollie had been alone for so long, it seemed to me they deserved some companionship. And happiness too. I was just glad to have been able to help them find it.

'Well, I guess we should let them get through their first date, first,' he went on, and I wasn't entirely sure if he was talking to me or himself. 'But there are worse stepdads to have than Ben, I suppose.'

That was true. As far as I was concerned, Gareth and Pollie would be lucky to have him – and him to have them. I meowed my enthusiastic agreement.

'I'm guessing that means sardines. Again.' Gareth sighed. 'Come on then, Lizzie, let's go.'

Lizzie? What sort of a name was *that*? Elizabeth was one thing, but I wasn't at all sure about *Lizzie*. One thing I was certain of, though, was that Ben and Pollie and Gareth had a chance here. One that none of them had probably even known they were looking for.

The chance to become a family.

Pollie and Gareth had been their own little family unit their whole lives, but I thought that expanding it could only be a good thing for all of them. Ben was a calm, understanding person who could help them repair their relationship after Gareth's running away. And when Gareth was ready to move out for real – he and Pollie had talked about him going to university, after all – then he wouldn't be leaving his mum alone.

DION LEONARD

They had a long way to go, I was sure. But I just had a feeling that everything would work out for this little family, at last. They'd probably let me stay, too, I realized. In fact, I knew they would. I was part of their family, too, in a way – I'd brought them together. But I knew that here – the bookshop, Australia, even – wasn't where I belonged.

I'd done what I'd run away to do. I'd travelled to new places, met new people, had new experiences ... and most of all, I'd helped people. But if my adventures had taught me anything, it was that the people who love us are the most important things in the world.

Mum and Dad and Gobi loved me – or they had. And I hoped they still did.

My work here was done and it was time to go home and find out for sure.

But how?

As I devoured my sardines, my thoughts turned to Jennifer. She'd been the first new human I'd met on my adventure, and looking back, I knew I wasn't the same cat I'd been when I met her.

Jennifer had helped me escape, taken me with her even after she realized I wasn't Cleo. She'd called in favours from a friend to help me travel safely – which I definitely hadn't appreciated the value of at the time. She'd taken me with her to her daughter's house, knowing they wouldn't want me there, then taken me out exploring the city with her. She'd needed me for companionship and support, and maybe someone to talk to who understood. Just like Anya and Ben had.

I just hadn't seen it then. I hadn't understood. I'd only considered her as a means to my own end – getting away for my adventure.

233

Now, though, I understood what Dad meant when he talked about Gobi helping him through the tough times in his race. About the comfort and companionship an animal can bring to a human. Before I'd run away, I'd thought it was the other way around – that I needed humans to feed me and take care of me. I'd repaid them in purrs and cuteness, but I hadn't considered that it went any deeper than that.

I knew now that my adventures weren't counted in the places I'd travelled to, or things I'd seen – but in the people I'd met and the lives I'd changed.

I'd given Ben and Pollie and Gareth and Anya and Harry – and even Jennifer – more than just a warm furry body to curl up with. I'd helped them find what they were looking for in life – well, except for Jennifer.

She'd been looking for the perfect place to finally lay her husband to rest. And I hadn't stayed long enough to help her find that. To repay her for everything she'd done for me.

She'd shown me the world – even if it was at the end of a harness.

Now I needed to help her too. At the very least, I couldn't let her fly home alone.

How long had I been in Australia? Too long, perhaps. Maybe Jennifer had already gone – taking with her my only hope of getting home, too.

But if she was still there …

It was time to leave. To go home, at last.

So, with one last mouthful of sardines, I sadly prepared myself to say goodbye to Ben's bookshop – and the family I'd found there – for ever.

Chapter
Nineteen

The next morning, I took a little extra time to savour the everyday comings and goings of the bookshop. Ben, sipping his coffee and reading the paper to me. Gareth banging through the door shortly after we opened, to ask about last night's date – then declaring he didn't need Ben to tell him anything: his mum's smile had told him everything he needed to know.

Ben's answering smile was full of secrets and hope. I watched it a moment too long, to make sure I never forgot what it looked like.

I made my final bowl of sardines last longer than usual, then took a small, restorative nap in my favourite sunny spot on the armchair, while Gareth continued reorganizing the bookshelves, shouting out the most ridiculous titles as he discovered them. He seemed to particularly delight in sharing ones from the large section of pink and purple coloured books, which all seemed to have something to do with love. I figured he was doing it mostly for the amusement of watching pink spots appear in Ben's cheeks.

I'd loved watching Gareth slowly bring the bookshop into order. It felt like between them, he and Ben were bringing the place back to life – finishing the process I'd started by drawing in new customers, and that Ben had taken on when he finally cleaned those grimy windows. The bookshop was getting a new lease of life, just as its owner was discovering the same thing for his *own* life.

Every day, the shop felt more and more like I'd thought it should since the day I arrived. It felt comfortable, homely, and right – a place I could stay for ever.

If a part of me wasn't already pulling towards the door.

This wasn't my place, however much it hurt to leave it behind. But eventually, I could put off leaving no longer.

I said goodbye to Ben and Gareth in my own way – winding around their legs until they petted me a little.

'You're very affectionate today, Elizabeth,' Ben observed, as he paused in sorting through another new box of books to scritch between my ears.

I didn't answer. Even if I could have spoken human, I don't think I'd have been able to find the words. Saying goodbye seemed to only get harder, every time I had to do it.

Finally, with a last look at the shop that had been my home for the last few weeks, I padded out through the open door, into the Sydney sunshine – just as I'd done so many times before.

Except this time, I wasn't coming back.

It took a little wandering around the city to retrace my steps back to the station I'd arrived at weeks before, but once I got there everything was straightforward and easy. A train swooped into the station just as I padded through the gates, and it was simple to hop up into the carriage with the crush of other passengers. I tucked myself away in the luggage rack and took a snooze on a soft holdall until I realized the train was starting to slow down. I didn't need to look out of windows, now, I knew where I was going: home.

As the train approached the station, though, I knew I needed to check where I was. Hopping down, I crossed to the nearest seat and reached up to lean against the window and look out.

(The person whose lap I was standing on didn't seem to mind too much.)

It was Jennifer's station! The one she'd brought me to that first day we'd explored the city together, and the one I'd caught the train from to get to Ben's. I'd hoped I'd remembered it right and got on a train going the right way, but the confirmation that I was on the right track was very reassuring. Jennifer would have said it was fate, I supposed.

With every step and paw-fall once I got off the train, I could feel myself growing closer to Jennifer – like she was pulling me in. I guessed that feeling must be something to do with that aura thing she was always talking about. No one else seemed to believe in it, but maybe it was enough that she did. Enough to draw me home, anyway.

No, not home. Not quite yet. But to the last stage of my adventure, at least.

Before I could go searching for Mum and Dad and Gobi, I had more work to do here in Australia, or on the next flight out. I needed to help Jennifer, the same way I'd helped Anya and Harry and Ben and Pollie and Gareth. *Then* I could go home.

And I hoped that Jennifer would help me get there. As long as she was still in the country, I was almost certain she would. But what if she'd gone? What if I was too late?

I'd soon find out. And the nearer I got, the more I needed to know.

The anticipation grew in my chest, a bubble of nervous impatience, and I started to walk faster and faster. I couldn't explain the sense of urgency that had come over me; I only knew that it was there, and that I needed to get to Jennifer as soon as I could. I picked up the pace even more and trotted faster, past Anya and Harry's school, past the shop where I'd met the alley cats (casting a nervous glance that way in case they were hanging around), past familiar trees and houses and landmarks until I was racing along the streets.

But as I careened around the corner to Jennifer's daughter's house, I realized why I'd felt the need to rush: I was almost too late! There was a taxi parked right outside, already loaded with what I recognized as Jennifer's bags and cases. She must have returned the hire car already. Panicked, I started to run faster than I ever had in my life. (Gobi and Dad's ultramarathoning had nothing on me!)

Nearly there. Nearly there, I kept repeating to myself in my head. I'd come too far to miss my last chance of getting home. I just had to keep running …

Skidding to a halt on the corner of the curb, I watched mother and daughter saying their goodbyes from a hidden spot behind a carefully trimmed shrub. *I'd made it!* Now I could catch my breath for a moment before revealing myself to Jennifer again.

'I really thought Fortune would have come back by now,' she was saying, tearfully, to Kitty on the doorstep. 'I was so sure she'd be here before I had to fly again.' Guilt sat heavily on my chest, hearing the distress in her voice. Poor Jennifer, I really hadn't understood what I was doing when I'd run away from her, without helping her first. But now I knew – and I was sorry.

'Mum, forget about the cat!' Kitty snapped. From her tone, and the way her arms were folded tight across her chest, I got the impression that Jennifer had spent quite a lot of time saying similar things since I'd left. I imagined this visit had been quite long enough for the both of them. It would probably be several more years again before they repeated it, I reckoned. 'It wouldn't be able to fly with you for the first leg anyway, remember?'

'I know, I know!' Jennifer moaned. 'But at least I'd know she was there with me, nearby in the hold. And I'd have her to comfort me when we landed, and for the next flight. I've missed her so much.'

Even at a distance, I could see Kitty rolling her eyes. 'We know. I think you missed her more than you ever miss us – your family – when you're on the other side of the world.'

'Now, Kitty, that's not true.' Jennifer looked hurt for a second, then a small smile appeared on her lips. 'Besides, if it were, that would only mean I'd need to visit more often. Build up that family bond between us.'

That got Kitty moving. 'Right, Mum, your cab is waiting! Don't want to run up the meter any more now, do you?'

But then, suddenly, they both seemed to have a last-minute change of heart – or maybe just a moment of regret that they hadn't made more of their visit together. I could see the change on their faces, and in their pace. They slowed right down next to the taxi door, and Jennifer rested her hand on Kitty's arm.

'I *do* miss you all, Kitty, very much,' she said, holding her daughter's gaze with her own. 'I know we might not always agree on everything—'

'Or *anything*,' Kitty interrupted, but there was a small smile on her lips that softened her words.

Jennifer returned the smile with one of her own. 'Perhaps not. But that doesn't mean that I love you any less than I ever have. Which is to say, totally, with my whole heart. You and the children – even John, really – you're all the family I have left, and I love you all and I miss you terribly. Even if it doesn't always seem that way.'

To my surprise, Kitty threw her arms around her mother and

held her tight. 'Oh, Mum! We all love you, too. We'll try and come and visit again soon, okay?'

'Maybe for Christmas?' Jennifer ventured, hopefully.

'Maybe. Next year, perhaps.'

'That would be lovely.'

Both smiling, they settled into the last-minute passport checks and another goodbye hug, plus promises to call soon. Realizing that if I didn't move quickly I really *would* miss my chance to get home, I hopped unseen into the boot of the taxi, burrowing in between the cases and my empty carrier.

It was much easier saying goodbye as a cat, I mused, as I waited for Jennifer to get in. Most of the time, the humans didn't even realize you were leaving, which helped. But it did mean you didn't get the hugs and the closure of a proper goodbye.

For the first time in my life, I was starting to realize how much I missed that. I'd have liked to have been able to say a *real* goodbye to Ben and Gareth, at least.

Finally, I heard the taxi door open, and Jennifer climb in. Should I jump out now and announce my presence, or wait until we reached the airport? I wasn't sure which was best. I didn't want to give Jennifer too much of a shock, as much as I knew she'd be pleased to see me!

While I was deliberating, the taxi driver struck up a conversation.

'Off to the airport? On holiday?' he asked, amiably.

I peered over the back of the nearest suitcase, just enough to see Jennifer in the back seat shake her head. 'Going home, at last.'

'Aw, right. Have a good trip?' I could see his eyes in the mirror, his gaze jumping between the road ahead and his passenger. Luckily, I blended so nicely with the cases, he didn't spot me.

'Most of it was great,' Jennifer replied, with a sigh. 'I got to see all sorts of sights, explore the city. And I spent a lot of quality time with my family.' She sighed again, heavily, and the driver's gaze hopped back to her face.

'So, what wasn't so great, then?' he asked. 'Because that sounds like a fantastic holiday to me!'

'Oh, it was!' Jennifer said, quickly. 'And I don't want to sound ungrateful, it's just …' From her handbag, she pulled the small, silver container she'd taken everywhere with her, while we'd been travelling together. 'I was supposed to be finding the perfect place to scatter my husband's ashes while I was here,' she explained. 'I promised him, before I died, that I'd travel the world until I found it. The ideal place for him to spend eternity. I was so sure it would be here, near my daughter and her family …'

'But you never felt that pull, huh?' the driver asked. 'That's tough.'

'You understand.' Jennifer gave a small, fleeting smile. 'Most people don't, you know. But worst of all, though, I lost my cat. She's the one thing that keeps me sane when I'm travelling, and now I have to make the whole trip back to Britain without her. I just don't know how I'm going to do it.'

The driver's gaze flickered up in the mirror again, and this time, I could tell that he saw me. A smile spread across his face.

'I'd take a look behind you, if I were you,' he said, grinning.

Frowning, Jennifer turned. This, I supposed, was my big moment! I stretched up, my paws on the top of the case, and meowed a welcome.

'Fortune!' Reaching behind her, she grabbed me and hauled me over the cases and into her arms, holding me tight against her chest, just like she had when the plane was taking off on our first trip together. It was sort of nice to be so appreciated, but also kind of uncomfortable, so after a minute I wiggled free again.

'I knew you wouldn't really leave me to fly home alone,' she murmured, as I settled onto her lap to let her stroke me. I felt a little guilty at that – I *had* almost left her alone. And if it hadn't been for Gareth and Pollie, not to mention the fact that she was my only way back out of the country, I might have done. But I'd come back, and she was pleased to see me. I'd help her find her own way home – and then I could find mine too. Once we were back in Britain, how hard could it be to find my way to Edinburgh?

Actually, how hard *would* it be? I had to admit that I had no idea. My safety net when I'd run away for my adventure had been my microchip. I didn't know *exactly* how they worked, but I knew that the little hard thing under my fur held all the information about my owners. If anything happened to me, if I got lost, humans could use it to reunite me with Mum and Dad.

I'd always had that as my back-up plan.

Except, of course, Jennifer had changed my microchip when we stopped in America. Whatever her vet friend had done – however dodgy it was – meant that my microchip said I belonged to *Jennifer* now. That I really was Fortune, not Lara.

How had I not realized before what this meant for my adventure? And my future, come to that?

It meant there was nothing in the world to tie me to Mum, Dad and Gobi any more. No way for anyone to know that I belonged with them, not Jennifer.

No way home, however many planes, trains and cars I travelled in.

My heart sank as the true horror of the situation sank in, finally.

I was Fortune, now.

And I might never be Lara, ever again.

 Gobi

Travelling in the hold of the plane to Australia was as terrible as last time had been, travelling across China. I'd thought that maybe because I knew what was coming, it wouldn't be so bad.

It was.

But it was all worth it, if it meant I got Lara back. Even the 10 days' quarantine in Melbourne was bearable, knowing that Dion and Lucja would be using the time to progress our search.

Finally, it was time for me to be allowed out into the country of Australia, and for us to carry on searching together. Except then, just when I thought the worst of it was over, things got more terrible than I could ever have imagined.

Dion had set up more interviews, in Sydney this time – and the schedule meant we needed to get there quickly. Which meant one more short flight in the cargo hold to get there from Melbourne.

'I'm so sorry, Gobi,' Dion said, as he checked me in at the freight terminal. I barked reassurances at him from inside my carrier. We were so close now, I'd do anything necessary to help find Lara.

But then, I did. And it was awful. And not just because of travelling in the hold, this time. That part went relatively fast. It was on the way out that trouble really started.

I was being carried out through the freight terminal, to where Dion and Lucja would be waiting for me, when I saw her: a Ragdoll cat in a hard-sided carrier, being taken through the freight terminal too, to the international area, ready for her own flight. I stared and stared – it couldn't be, could it?

But then I heard her meow in protest as her carrier was jostled, and I knew without a doubt that it was.

It was Lara. My Lara.

I barked up a storm, desperately trying to get her attention, but her carrier was facing the wrong way now, she couldn't see me. I tried calling her name, but she was already gone, away through the doors that led to her plane – and away from me. Leaving me behind with a million questions.

Like: what did we do now? What was the point in searching Sydney for Lara, of all the TV interviews Dion had set up, now I knew she'd already left the country?

How could I ever explain what I'd seen to Dion and Lucja when we didn't even speak the same language?

And, most of all, where was Lara going next?

Even though I knew Lara wasn't there, I still had to do the TV appearances, trying to get the Australian people to look out for my sister. I just hoped that she was out there somewhere, watching us. That she knew how hard we were searching for her. How much we missed her.

And I hoped whichever humans she was with – if she was even with humans, although I assumed she must be, to be travelling on another plane – watched it too, wherever they'd travelled to. That they called and told us where she was.

I hoped that Dion was right, and that she was still with Jennifer. At least then I had faith that if she saw one of our TV interviews, or spotted an article in a magazine or newspaper, she *would call. Surely she must have realized by now Lara wasn't Cleo?*

With every day that passed without a phone call, I could tell that Dion and Lucja were growing more and more despondent. Getting out to Australia – through the flights and the immigration hoops and the quarantine – had seemed like the biggest challenge. I think we'd all hoped that once we arrived, things would be easy. That Lara would be at the airport waiting to meet us, even.

Of course, that didn't happen. She'd been there – just not for us. She'd already been leaving again. Not that they knew that.

But finally, finally, one day shortly after we arrived, we got a call.

'He says he owns a bookshop in Sydney, and had a cat that matched Lara's description hanging around for a few weeks,' Dion said, as he put down the phone.

'Is she still there?' Lucja was on her feet before he'd even finished talking.

But Dion shook his head. 'She disappeared a few days ago, apparently. But it's not far. I thought we could head over, talk to him, see if it really was Lara – he says he has a photo of her.'

'And if it was her, maybe she'll come back,' Lucja suggested. 'Especially if he was feeding her.'

'Exactly what I was thinking,' Dion said. 'Come on, Gobi, time for a walk.' He shook my harness, and I raced across the hotel room to put it on.

As Dion had promised, the bookshop wasn't too far to walk from our hotel. Lucja pushed open the door, making a bell tinkle. Inside, books were stacked everywhere, like a library had been emptied into the shop unsorted, and there was a teenage boy behind the counter.

'Um, we're here to see Ben?' Dion said. 'It's about a cat.'

'Lizzie, right,' the boy said, cheerfully. 'Hang on, Ben's just in the kitchen.' He disappeared through a door, and we heard him say,

'Seriously, don't you two ever stop kissing? It's vile! And there are some people and a dog wanting to talk to you about Elizabeth, anyway.'

Dion and Lucja exchanged a look, and Dion mouthed, Elizabeth? in a disbelieving manner.

I wasn't so sure. I could see Lara as an Elizabeth – she had that Queen of the World quality that suited royal names.

A tousled-looking man in brown trousers appeared through the door. 'Hi! I'm Ben. I guess you must be Dion and Lucja?'

'That's right. You say you think our cat might have been staying with you?' Dion got right down to the important matters, as usual.

Ben nodded. 'Yeah. Hang on, there's a photo of her here …' He pulled a poster with a picture of a Ragdoll cat out from a stack of paperwork on the desk. I couldn't see enough to be sure if it was Lara or not, but I didn't need to – I could smell her scent all through the shop.

Dion and Lucja both studied the photo carefully, though – their noses aren't as useful as mine.

'It definitely looks like her,' Lucja said. 'And you have no idea where she came from?'

Ben shook his head. 'None at all. Except for a while, I had this photo of her in the window, inviting people in to meet the bookshop cat. And after she disappeared again, I put up a "missing" poster with the same photo. While that was up, a young girl came in – I think she said her name was Anya. Hang on, she left her number …' he rummaged around again on the desk and pulled out another scrap of card. 'Yes, Anya. She said she'd had a cat just like Elizabeth staying in her tree house for a week or so, just before Elizabeth arrived here at the bookshop. She obviously hadn't gone back there when Anya came by, but she might have done since?'

'Can I take this?' Dion asked, reaching for the card with the phone number on it. 'I'd like to give Anya a call, see if she can shed any more light on Lara's adventures.'

'Lara.' Ben smiled. 'That's a good name for her, too. And, yes, of course. Just let me copy it down for you …'

Dion had unclipped my harness when we stopped in the shop, so I let the humans talk, while Ben hunted for a pen and another piece of paper. I wanted to follow up the trail of Lara's scent, instead.

She'd definitely spent a lot of time there, I had no doubt of that. I sniffed at the floor, following the scent trail around the shop. She'd been everywhere, it seemed, but it seemed most heavily focussed on the armchair by the door – and a small pile of cushions in the corner of the brightly coloured section filled with picture books.

Desperate to be close to even just somewhere Lara had been, I burrowed into the cushions. And that was where I found it.

Tugging it out by the cover with my teeth, I dragged the book across to where the humans were still talking, and laid it at Dion's feet.

'Where did you find that?' he asked, as he picked up the copy of my book, with my picture on the front.

I woofed, and raced back to the pile of cushions to show him.

'That's where Elizabeth slept some nights,' Ben said, in amazement. 'I think it was warmer than the armchair she napped on during the day.'

Dion turned the book over in his hands. 'That settles it, then. Lara was definitely here.'

'The question is, where is she now?' Lucja asked.

We were all thinking the same thing as we walked back to the hotel. But little did we know there was one more phone call to come … One that would change everything.

Chapter
Twenty

One advantage of having my microchip fixed, and matched to Cleo's passport, was that it meant getting out of the country was easy, at least. And I didn't have to serve any time in quarantine flying *out* of Australia, although I wasn't looking forward to the first flight in the hold of the plane.

Jennifer wasn't looking forward to being apart from me again either, I could tell. As we waited for me to be checked and taken in at the freight terminal, she told me all about the adventures she'd had while I'd been away. I wished I was able to share mine, too, but I knew Jennifer – for all her intuition and auras – wouldn't understand my meows.

The first flight was miserable, cold and lonely – as expected. I hunkered down and focussed on the destination, rather than the journey, for a change. Soon, I'd be home again. Somehow. I had to keep believing that.

We changed flights again – in Hong Kong this time, and without an emergency stop at the vet's – and for the next flight, I was able to sit with Jennifer in the cabin of the plane. She cuddled me tight through take-off, and I found myself wondering about Cleo, and whether she'd managed to stay hidden at the airport or not.

Had she escaped from my carrier, leaving Mum, Dad and Gobi behind? Or – and I shuddered as the thought occurred to me – had she stayed with them, usurping my place altogether? Pretending to be me, even?

She wouldn't do that to me – would she?

I shook my head to drive away these dark thoughts – I needed to focus on the important things instead.

Like getting home to Mum and Dad. And Gobi.

Would they be happy to see me again? I hoped so.

Across the aisle, I caught the eye of another emotional support animal – this one a small dog, not unlike Gobi. His owner was clutching him tightly, too, so we exchanged a look of shared understanding.

'I hate these flights,' he said. 'Don't you?'

I stretched out my paws in front of me, nonchalantly. 'I've had worse.' This dog had clearly never travelled in the hold of a plane before. 'You should try travelling to Australia. Nice country, but the quarantine is the pits!'

'You been to a lot of places, then?' the dog asked.

I smiled secretively. 'A few. But right now, it's nice to be going home. How long until we land in France, do you know?' I knew we wouldn't be flying into Britain; Jennifer would want me with her for as much of the journey as possible. I was a seasoned traveller now. It felt good knowing these things, and not having to rely on someone else to tell me.

Except apparently, I didn't know *everything* about travelling, just yet.

'France?' the dog huffed a laugh, clearly no longer impressed by my travelling credentials. 'This plane isn't going to *France*, sweetheart. We're on our way to China!'

China? Wait, that wasn't right. We were meant to be going *home*!

Or … or maybe it was fate, again, following Jennifer around and acting to make things work out for the best. Because Mum and Dad and Gobi had been flying to China too … Maybe they were still there? Could that be possible? I had no idea how long they'd planned on staying – and no truly accurate idea of how long I'd been gone, either.

Still, by the time we landed in Beijing, I'd convinced myself that of course my family would still be there. This was meant to be. I had a feeling, just like Jennifer got feelings. Certainties, even.

Everything would be fine. Probably.

'Oh, this is going to be wonderful, I can tell!' Jennifer said, as we settled into our hotel room. It wasn't anything fancy, but apparently finding hotels willing to take pets had been a challenge. 'A whole week here in Beijing to explore the city, learn about the culture. My Jeremy would have loved it. He always wanted to come here. You know, Fortune, I'm hoping maybe this city will provide the final resting place for him that I've been searching for for so long.'

I hoped so too, for her sake – and for Cleo's too. She'd been travelling and looking for too long already. I was sure that once she was reunited with Cleo – which I'd convinced myself she would be, somehow – both Jennifer *and* her pet would enjoy some peaceful time at home together. In fact, after all my adventures, even *I* was looking forward to some time sat behind a window, watching the rest of the world go about its business. And eating prawns, of course.

I was *really* looking forward to prawns for dinner every night again.

That would definitely mean I was home.

Jennifer didn't waste any time. Before she was even unpacked, she had me on my harness, ready to explore the city streets. I was starting to feel that I'd done enough exploring for one year, and I was none too keen on going back to doing it while bound into a harness after my weeks of freedom, but Jennifer seemed so excited that I didn't like to make a fuss.

'I've got tours and trips planned for the other days,' she told me, as we headed down to the hotel lobby. 'Lots of wonderful places I'm sure Jeremy would have just loved. But today, I just want to get a feel for the city. Then we can come back and have a drink in the bar and something to eat. Sound good?'

Well, I liked the 'something to eat' part, anyway, so I meowed my agreement.

From cat level, Beijing was much like any other city. Concrete under paw, lights up above, and too many legs getting in my way. The colours seemed brighter than back home though, the signs more lit up and plentiful. There were lots of shops, lots of music, lots of sound. There were market stalls too, selling what Jennifer called 'street food' – which smelled delicious. I kept hoping one of the stallholders would take pity on a hungry cat and toss me a snack, but they didn't.

When I looked up, the buildings towered higher than any I'd ever seen before, looming grey against the sky. Many of them were boring next to the brightly coloured and flashing signs hanging from the shops, closer to my own level.

I didn't understand the language anyone was speaking, and even if I had been able to read, I don't think I could have made sense of the signs I saw. Everything felt so very different from home, or even Australia. It wasn't a bad different, exactly, I just didn't know how to understand it yet. Maybe after a few days here I'd feel more at home – especially if I'd found my family by then.

So, instead of trying to make sense of the things around me as Lara – or Fortune – I tried to imagine it through Gobi's eyes instead. This was where Gobi was from, after all – this country, if not this city. This was where Gobi and Dad had lived, for all those months before he was allowed to bring Gobi home to live with us.

Gobi had told me stories of the time they spent there. The apartment they lived in, the shops nearby, the canal they walked along, the food – especially something she said was called a Beijing Burrito.

She'd even talked about the vet who operated on her hurt leg, and her terror when, at the airport after long months waiting until she was allowed to fly home with Dad, it looked for a time like she wouldn't be permitted aboard the plane because of a mistake with the paperwork. (After all my travels, I could see much more clearly now how that might have happened!) But she'd never talked about what happened when she was missing. Not once. Which made me think that her adventures in this city alone must have been a lot less fun than mine had been, over in Australia.

I couldn't wait to tell Gobi everything that *I'd* been up to.

But first, I had to find them again.

So, as we walked the streets, I kept my eyes wide open, look-ing for Gobi. If they *were* still in the city, I'd see them, I was sure. Yes, Beijing was a big place – huge, even. But I had faith. Everything else had fallen into place so well on my adventure, it seemed only right that this would too.

Or maybe I'd just been spending too much time with Jennifer, to be putting my faith in fate that way.

In truth, it was hard to imagine my family there – now, or back then, when it was just Dad and Gobi. It wasn't home for them, any more than it was for me. But I had to hope that they were still there. Otherwise I had no idea how I was going to find them.

But fate, Jennifer said sometimes, could be tricky.

We turned the corner onto another big street, packed with people and smattered with well-spread out trees, just like the last one. And as with the last street, I scanned the area for any sign of my family, which was when I spotted a row of shop windows up ahead. They were filled with TVs again, just like the one I'd seen in Sydney. And suddenly, suddenly, there they were.

My family. Once again, displayed on an oversized TV screen.

Except this time, they were holding up a photo.

A photo of *me*.

Desperate, I tried to pull Jennifer closer, but she'd been distracted by something across the street, and was already moving the other way. I tugged on the harness, but to no avail – I wasn't strong enough to change her path.

'Come on, Fortune, the lights have changed!' She dragged me with her across the road.

I stared behind me the whole way, at the picture of my family together on the screen, my photo in the corner. I drank in the sight of them again after so long.

I want to come home, I thought to them, wishing that they could somehow hear my message and come rescue me. Then I blinked, just before they were out of sight. There was something else about the image on the screen. Something that looked oddly familiar …

And I realized suddenly what was behind them, out of the window of the TV studio.

The shells of the roof of the Sydney Opera House, looking just as they had when I'd explored Sydney with Jennifer.

My family weren't in China any longer, they were in Australia! *In the city I'd only just left!*

I trailed miserably after Jennifer as she continued exploring the city, trying to figure out the meaning behind what I'd just seen. It didn't make any sense.

The Opera House was easy: my family had gone to Australia. But why? Now I knew how hard it was to get an animal into the country. Gobi would have had to travel in the hold, and go through quarantine and everything! I couldn't imagine Mum and Dad putting her through that just for a couple of interviews on TV.

And then there was the photo of me, shown in the corner of the screen, above the strange writing that scrolled along the bottom. Had they been talking about me?

More importantly, had they been *looking* for me?

I'd not even been certain that they'd miss me at all. I'd been so sure they were carrying on their normal lives with Gobi, without me. Book tours, TV interviews, they did that sort of thing all the time. But not with a photo of me.

The idea that they were going on TV, asking people if they'd seen me … it seemed impossible. But it was also the only logical explanation for what I'd seen.

It left me feeling confused and uncertain, like there was a big hole in the middle of my belly that no amount of prawns could fill.

And one question kept echoing around in my head.

Now what did I do?

When we finally returned to the hotel room, I jumped up at the TV on the wall, trying to persuade Jennifer to turn it on, desperate to see if my family were still there, still searching. But she only laughed.

'We won't understand anything they're showing anyway, Fortune. Unless we can find a cat channel!' she joked.

With another giggle, she headed off into the bathroom to get ready for dinner, leaving me alone and despondent.

Somehow I needed to get her to realize my family were searching for me. But how? More than ever before, I wished I could talk human. Before, it would have been useful. Now, it was vital!

By the time we headed down to the hotel bar for dinner, I was starting to lose all hope. Even the promise from Jennifer that she'd order something delicious to share with me couldn't cheer me up. What were prawns, compared to my family? I sulked, and refused to even look at the food the waiters brought.

That was, until I saw the TV in the corner of the bar.

Fate had intervened again.

The TV was on. And the programme it was showing looked a bit like the one I'd seen earlier. Even here, in another country, I could recognize the format of what Dad called 'The News'.

I watched avidly as Jennifer ate, waiting to see if my family would appear again. It was probably too much to hope for, but I couldn't help myself: this might be my last chance to find a way home.

Then, suddenly, there they were – just as I'd seen them that afternoon.

Meowing loudly, I jumped forward, up onto the bar and over to the TV.

'Fortune!' Jennifer called, lurching after me, trying to grab me around the middle.

But I eluded her, and raced across the surface of the bar, until my nose was pressed up against the TV – and the picture of me on it.

'What on earth are you …? Oh!' Jennifer stopped, stared at the TV, and turned white. 'Oh. Oh no! Those poor, poor people! Of course! Why didn't I realize …?' She reached over the bar and grabbed a pen from the bartender's hand. 'Sorry, I need this.'

Taking a small napkin from the pile on the bar, Jennifer scribbled down the series of numbers scrolling across the screen.

'Come on, Fortune. No, *not* Fortune.' She looked at me, shaking her head a little sadly. 'You're Lara, aren't you?'

I purred my enthusiastic agreement. I'd been starting to think I might never hear my *real* name again!

'Well, come on then, Lara. We need to make a phone call.' She checked her watch. 'I have no idea what time it is in Australia right now, but I don't think your family will mind being woken up, do you?'

Chapter
Twenty-One

After that, things became unexpectedly simple. One phone call – and a lot of shrieking on the other end, from what I could hear – and my life became my own again. I was Lara once more. Not Cleo or Fortune, or Puss or Elizabeth, or even the hated *Lizzie*. Just Lara.

But not the Lara who'd sat behind windows and watched other people exploring the world outside. I was Lara the Runaway Cat – who had travelled the world having adventures, helping people, changing lives and making a difference.

And now, all I wanted in the world was to go home, with my family.

It took a couple of days after the initial phone call for Mum, Dad and Gobi to arrive in China.

'Flight times,' Jennifer explained. 'Plus, they had to cancel a few interviews, I think. And Dion said something about needing to call someone called Ben to let him know you'd been found …'

Ben! How on earth had Mum and Dad met him? I had no idea. But I was beyond grateful that he, at least, wouldn't have to wonder for ever what had happened to me. Maybe my family would say a proper goodbye to him and Gareth and Pollie for me.

Finally, though, we got word that their plane had landed in Beijing, and Jennifer and I headed downstairs to wait impatiently for them to arrive at the hotel.

'Lara!' Mum raced across the lobby and swept me up into her arms, harness and all, followed by Dad, who wrapped his arms around both of us. At their feet, Gobi barked happily, and I knew she was pleased to see me again.

And I was strangely happy to see her, too. I'd expected the rush of pleasure and reassurance that flooded me as soon as I saw Mum and Dad. But I hadn't expected to be quite so relieved and pleased to have that troublesome interloper Gobi back in my life.

I'd missed her, I realized. A lot. Far more than I'd ever dreamt I would. Maybe even more than I'd missed Mum and Dad.

It was strange, but in some ways it felt like she'd been on my adventure with me, every step of the way. I'd thought of her so often – imagining what she'd have done, or how my escapades matched up to hers – it was almost as if she'd been there beside me through my many plane trips, my adventures around Australia, and definitely here in Beijing. But in the end, the truth remained – I'd been alone, apart from the new friends I'd made on the way. And I'd learned that while adventures could be great fun, they simply weren't as good as family.

Dad put me down on the floor to greet Gobi, and I brushed up against her, reacquainting myself with her scent, her feel, and rubbing my fluffy tail across her back the way she always liked. It felt so, so good to be close to her again.

Not that I was planning on letting on to *her* how much I'd missed her – it would only go to her head after all.

'I can't believe we found you!' Gobi yapped, excitedly.

'Oh, were you looking?' I said, as nonchalantly as I could manage, given all the emotions surging through me. 'Sorry, I was too busy having adventures to notice.'

Gobi just rolled her eyes good-naturedly.

'I'm so, so sorry!' Jennifer said to Mum as she hugged her. 'By the time I realized she wasn't Cleo, I was already halfway to

Australia. And even then, I didn't put it together and realize what must have happened! So stupid of me, really. But I was in such a flap about flying, and then about losing Cleo and … Well, to be honest, I sort of thought it must be a sign. That Fortune – I mean Lara – had been sent to help me with my search. It never occurred to me that you would be searching for *her*.'

Mum and Dad exchanged a look. I was fairly sure they were silently agreeing on Jennifer's craziness.

I wound myself around Jennifer's legs in support. She might be a little out there, but she'd helped me: she'd brought me home – to my family.

'I don't suppose you know what *did* happen to Cleo?' Jennifer asked. 'It's been bothering me ever since we left Paris. I mean, I know she can take care of herself – she's a very clever cat, you know. But still, I did worry …'

'Why don't we get a drink at the bar,' said Dad, 'and we'll tell you the whole story – and you can tell us yours?'

'We're desperate to know what Lara has been up to while we've been apart,' Mum added. 'We've managed to piece some of it together from people we've spoken to – which reminds me, Dion, we need to call Ben and Anya to let them know we've been reunited with Lara.'

Ben *and* Anya! How on earth had my family found *both* of them? I hoped Gobi would be able to tell me later, but for now I was just glad that all my friends knew I was safe.

'Yes, it seems that Lara has had all sorts of adventures without us,' Dad said. 'But we'd love to hear about *your* travels with her.'

Jennifer looked down at me. 'Well, I'll tell you what I know, too. But to be honest, I think *Lara* might be the only one who knows the truth about *all* her adventures!'

★ ★ ★

That night, I curled up with Gobi in Mum and Dad's hotel room to sleep, happy to be with my family again. I wondered how Jennifer was coping without me, back in her own hotel room. We'd stayed up talking with her until late, and it seemed that between them, the humans had all managed to piece together *most* of my travels. Not all, of course, but then they were only human!

In return for Jennifer's stories, Mum and Dad had told her the tale of Cleo's escape, and how the airport had found her and were looking after her until they could get in touch with Jennifer. It seemed to me that it had all gone according to Cleo's plan – until it got to them checking her microchip, anyway.

'Oh, those blasted microchips!' Jennifer had said. 'More trouble than they're worth, sometimes. Jeremy was always in charge of those. I suppose he must have put *his* mobile number as the main contact, and I never thought to change it after he died!'

She'd told Mum and Dad about me, too. All the things I'd seen and places I'd been with her. Gobi had looked a little impressed, I'd thought. Mum had just cuddled me tighter again.

'Tell me the rest of it,' Gobi said sleepily, as we snuggled on Dad's bed. 'What happened after you left Jennifer? I mean, we know you stayed with Anya and with Ben, but even they couldn't account for *all* the time you were gone.'

'You really want to know?' I asked.

Gobi nodded. 'I want to know *everything* about your adventures.'

So, I told her everything. All about Jennifer's daughter and the alley cats, all about Anya, Harry and Petra, and all about the bookshop, Ben, Gareth and Pollie.

'We went there,' Gobi said, her eyes already mostly closed. 'Dion just called Anya, so I never saw the tree house, but we did go there. The bookshop, I mean. They seemed like nice people there.'

'They were,' I said. Then, when I was certain she was asleep, I added, 'But nobody else is as good as family, sister.'

At the end of the week, we all flew back to France – where Jennifer retrieved a well-rested and relaxed Cleo from the quarantine area she'd been kept in for safe-keeping.

'You made it back, then,' Cleo said, looking faintly impressed. 'I wasn't sure you would.'

'Neither was I,' I admitted. 'Did you have fun hanging out at the airport?'

'It was better than flying again.'

'Not for me.' I thought of all the adventures I'd had, and the joy I'd felt as my first plane had soared through the skies. 'Still, I'm glad to be going home again.'

'Me too,' Cleo agreed.

We exchanged one more smug look at the success of our plans, before we were put back in our carriers to get back in the car.

From there, we drove to somewhere called Calais and then caught the ferry back home together – a different, shorter crossing to the one we'd taken over to France all those many weeks before. There was no cabin with beds this time, just some seats we commandeered and sat around in talking.

It was strange to think that I might never see Jennifer again after this. Although I was pleased to be reunited with my family, I was also a little sad to have to say goodbye to all the friends I'd made along the way. At least I knew that I'd helped them all be a little happier, and get what they wanted most in the world.

All except Jennifer. I frowned as I saw her sitting opposite us on the ferry, sighing as she looked out of the window. Yes, I'd helped her fly home, and together we'd reunited her with Cleo. But she still hadn't found the perfect place to scatter her husband's ashes. The one thing she'd been travelling the world for in the first place.

How could she ever settle down again if she couldn't fulfil her promise to Jeremy?

'I think I might go for a little walk around the deck,' Jennifer said, her voice sounding far away. Cleo was curled up asleep in her carrier. 'May I leave Cleo with you?'

'Of course,' Mum said. 'If you trust us not to lose her again!'

Jennifer didn't need to be concerned about that, I knew. Now she didn't have to go on another plane for a while, Cleo would be happy to stay with her owner again.

Until Jennifer thought of somewhere else that Jeremy might like to spend eternity, of course.

With a quick glance behind me, I snuck away to follow Jennifer up onto the deck. This might be my last chance to help her, and I didn't want to pass it up. I wasn't sure what I could *do* exactly, but I hoped that fate might give me a hint.

It only took me a moment to find Jennifer. She was stood at the rail of the ship, staring out at the sea as it stretched away for miles and miles. Cautiously, I hopped up onto the ledge beside her, keeping a careful eye on the waves below. The last thing I wanted was to fall overboard, not when I was so close to home!

'Hello, Fortune.' Jennifer smiled down at me, as she petted my head. 'I can still call you that when it's just the two of us, can't I?'

I supposed I didn't mind too much. Somehow, it felt like I wasn't *just* Lara any more – I was Fortune and Puss and Elizabeth, too. So, I meowed my agreement, which made Jennifer sigh.

'You always did seem to understand just what I was trying to say.' Keeping one hand on my back, she stared back out at the water. 'I was just thinking about my dear Jeremy ... I never did find the right place to scatter these.' She pulled the small silver box from her bag. 'I keep thinking about how he would have loved all these adventures – but he'd have wanted to go home too. He loved Britain, more than anywhere else in the world. He always said he felt most at home when he could see the Cliffs of Dover approaching, and he knew he was nearly back in Blighty – a hang on from his days in the Navy, I suppose ... Wait!'

Suddenly, everything about her was tense and stiff. I tensed too, my back arched, looking for danger.

Then I realized – Jennifer wasn't afraid, she was *excited*.

Her eyes widened, and she pointed out ahead of the boat. 'See there! Those white splodges in the distance – that's Dover! Why didn't I ever think of it before? Well, I know why – I always stayed inside with Cleo on ferries. She never liked coming up near the waves, so I never looked out before ... But now ...' She turned to me, joy colouring her cheeks. 'This is it, Fortune! This is the place I've been looking for all along!'

Then, with tears rolling down her cheeks and a smile spreading across her whole face, Jennifer opened that little silver box and scattered the contents out over the waves.

'Rest well, my love,' she whispered. 'You can see home from here.'

I pressed against her side in support and, once she was done, Jennifer gathered me close.

'Thank you, Lara,' she murmured in my ear. 'For helping *both* of us find home again.'

I purred. I'd really done it – I'd helped her after all, in the end. My work here was finished.

It was time to go home, at last.

 # Gobi

When Lara and Jennifer came back inside the ferry, something in me relaxed. Somehow, I knew that Lara's adventures were done, at last, as she curled up next to me again.

She might pretend she hadn't missed us, or that coming home again was no big deal. But I'd found my book in that shop, by where she slept, and it was covered in her scent – like a favourite toy or comforter. She'd missed us.

But she'd changed too, while she'd been gone. I could see it in the way she cared for Jennifer, in the way she talked about the people she'd met on her travels. This Lara cared more about people than she had. She wanted to support and help them. And not just as a way to get more prawns.

I liked this Lara a lot.

I'd missed her so much when she was gone. She was family, every bit as much as Dion and Lucja are, and the world wasn't as friendly or fun when she wasn't nearby.

Ever since we'd received Jennifer's phone call, back in Sydney, we'd been racing to put our family back together. And now, I knew we'd done it at last. Whatever had driven Lara to escape on her adventures, it was over: she'd found what she needed to and done what she felt she had to do.

I hoped one day she'd tell me the full story of that. Not just the details of where she'd been, or what had happened to her. I wanted to know more than the facts.

I wanted to understand why she'd run away in the first place, and what had changed her so profoundly into the cat who came home again.

But I could wait. Lara was back with us, and we were a family again – that meant I had all the time in the world to find out her secrets.

Still, it didn't hurt to make sure of that …

As she fell asleep, I stood guard over her. Now she was back with us, I wasn't going to risk losing her again. Not ever.

We are a family. And family sticks together.

Through everything – even adventures.

Chapter
Twenty-Two

It was late and dark and we were all exhausted, but we had finally arrived. Too many planes, ferries and car rides later, we were back.

Home again at last. All of us, together.

The house in Edinburgh looked just as I remembered it, filled with all the familiar things I loved. The pictures on the walls, photos of Dad and Mum and Gobi and me. The chair, where Dad and I sat to watch TV together. My bed, where Gobi always wanted to sleep, too. My squeaky ball. The garden outside the back door, with its butterflies and birds, and grass for chewing. Everything I'd left behind – and worried I might never see again.

It was all there waiting for me. Just like my family had been.

I took a moment to explore, and reacquaint myself with the place, before returning to the lounge to sit by my window and watch the world outside.

As I sat, I thought back over my adventures. All the people and animals I'd met along the way – from the ones who'd taken me in and loved me, to the alley cats who'd shown me how hard life is alone, to the statue of a Queen's dog, who'd helped me to understand the importance of helping others.

Everything might be the same back home in Edinburgh, but *I* definitely wasn't the same cat who'd left this house weeks ago, hoping for an adventure. And most of that change was down to all the people I'd met on my travels.

I wished I had a way to thank them. Mum and Dad had spoken again to Ben and Anya, I knew, and promised to email them photos of me back home. Jennifer, too, had left her details – and even promised to pop in if she was ever in Edinburgh. But I knew there was a very real chance I'd never see the people who'd changed my life ever again, and that made me a little sad.

A little sadness couldn't outweigh my happiness at being home again, though.

Dad brought me an extra-big bowl of prawns, which I devoured quickly. (I had really, *really* missed prawns!) Still, I couldn't help but glance back outside, again and again.

Beyond the window, life in Edinburgh went on, even so late at night. There were humans and animals and noises and cars and scents and everything, just beyond the window. Lives being lived, adventures being had.

And as I watched, I realized something important.

I couldn't stay behind windows for the rest of my life, not now I knew what was out there. So many things to see and people to meet. Lives to change and people to help.

I'd have more adventures, I was sure of it.

But from now on, wherever I went, whatever I saw, whoever I met and whatever I did – I'd always make sure I knew the way back home again.

And I'd always be home in time for tea.

Acknowledgements

I 'd like to thank Oliver Malcolm from HarperCollins UK for his initial ideas on the book, his belief in the project and his ongoing support. Thanks to co-writer Sophie Pembroke for her wonderful creative thoughts, vision and hard work in bringing the story to life. Thanks to Vicky Eribo from HarperCollins UK for her help, patience and guidance. A shout out to all the *Finding Gobi* followers around the world who continue to support and encourage us to continue sharing Gobi's true story and our amazing journey together since. Thanks to Lisa Anderson who has helped us out massively over the years looking after Lara – we appreciate everything you've done for us and so does Lara, even if she doesn't show it! Finally, to all the prawn farmers of the world, we salute you – without you our lives would not be the same!